Heart Animals

PET CHAPLAIN LEARNING SERIES • VOLUME 1

Heart Animals

Sacred Stories About the Special Pets Who Change Our Lives

Rob Gierka, EdD
Karen Duke

Pet Chaplain® Learning Series

VOLUME 1

Heart Animals
Sacred Stories About Pets Who Change Our Lives

VOLUME 2

Always in My Heart
Coping Creatively with Pet Loss

VOLUME 3

Just an Animal
Reflections on the Human-Animal Bond
and Western Culture

VOLUME 4

Veterinary Chaplaincy
Interfaith Spiritual Care for Pet Loss

Visit petchaplain.com to learn more about the series
and other resources available from Pet Chaplain.

This book is dedicated to the unsung heroes
of the veterinary world—the hardworking vet techs
who provide amazing care to our
beloved animal companions.

If I can stop one heart from breaking,

I shall not live in vain;

If I can ease one life the aching,

Or cool one pain,

Or help one fainting robin

Unto his nest again,

I shall not live in vain.

— Emily Dickinson, *Poems*

Contents

A Note from the Authors

Welcome to the Pet Chaplain Learning Series! I'm Rob Gierka, founder and president of Pet Chaplain, and I'll be your guide for this unique learning experience. In this introductory note, I'll provide some essential information about the series, including an overview of its goals and recommendations for engaging with the books.

This book is the first volume in a four-book set that explores pet keeping and loss in contemporary Western society. If you're passionate about pets, concerned with the well-being of all animals, or simply curious about the human-animal bond, you'll learn a great deal about this remarkable social and cultural phenomenon with this series. If you've recently lost a pet and are struggling with grief—or if you're thinking about a pet lost years before—you'll find the support you need within one or all of the first three books in the series. These volumes examine pet keeping and loss from different angles so you can explore your experience holistically. The fourth book in the series builds on the content of the first three books with a focus on interfaith spiritual care for pet loss, providing an invaluable resource for caregiving professionals and others interested in this new field of spiritual care.

The series addresses four primary questions: Why are our animal companions so important to us? How do we navigate the deep sorrow we experience as we rebuild our lives without their physical presence? How do our social interactions impact our journey of grief when we lose our pets? And how can we best help each other find lasting peace and a renewed sense of purpose? The series explores these queries through a combination of scholarship and storytelling that vividly capture the lived reality of pet keeping and loss in the modern West.

Regarding scholarship, the series takes a broad, interdisciplinary approach. It draws on many academic disciplines, including human-animal studies, clinical psychology, existential psychology, death studies, philosophy, sociology, anthropology, religious studies, history, and neuroscience. This holistic approach is increasingly rare in today's siloed academic world, where most scholars focus solely on their area of expertise. Yet life is not easily divided into neat categories, and I've taken considerable care to synthesize the research cited in the series into a holistic perspective of our complex and continually evolving relationship with the greater-than-human world. Geographically, however, I've had to limit my research because it was impractical to incorporate scholarship for locations outside the West. Most of the research about pet keeping and loss, the human experience of grief, and other topics covered in the series is based on studies conducted in the US and, to a lesser extent, Canada, Australia, and Western Europe.

To balance out all this scholarship, the series includes an abundance of pet stories. These narratives are important not only because people love to read stories but because stories are critical to a good education. There's an old proverb that says: "Tell me the facts, and I'll learn. Tell me the truth, and I'll believe. But tell me a story and it will live in my heart forever." When you've read everything I have to say about pet keeping and loss, I expect it's the stories you'll remember best.

Many voices make an appearance in the series. I tell my own stories about pets I've loved and lost as well as the pivotal experiences that have shaped my interest in this new field of spiritual care. You'll read the stories of pet keepers who attended my pet loss support group over the last two decades. You'll gain insight into the veterinary world as I reflect on my service as the on-call chaplain at a large veterinary teaching hospital. You'll read the stories and reflections of people who participated in an online course in veterinary chaplaincy that my co-author Karen Duke and I developed and taught for five years. Finally, you'll discover the amazing insights offered by a small group of aspiring veterinary technologists ("vet techs") who I interviewed for my doctoral research study of the human-animal bond and bereavement.

The four volumes that comprise the series are not textbooks per se, or at least not the kind of textbook you may have read before. As an educational program, the series is modeled on the self-paced courses offered by the Great Books Foundation, a nonprofit organization that promotes lifelong learning through reading and discussion of literature, philosophy, poetry, and other compelling texts. For fourteen years, I participated in a Great Books discussion group with a small group of well-read and highly accomplished octogenarians. It was one of the best learning experiences of my life, and I've long wanted to create a rich, transformative learning experience for others.

One of the series' greatest strengths—and the quality that sets it apart from other books about pet keeping and loss—is its wealth of learning resources. The first three books in the series include thought-provoking questions that encourage critical engagement with many concepts related to pet keeping and loss, giving you the opportunity to articulate your beliefs on a variety of animal-related topics. There are no "right" answers to these questions. Rather, their goal is to promote critical thinking, exploration, analysis, and the clear articulation of your personal perspective on the diverse topics explored in the series. The more time and effort you put into this work, the more you'll learn about yourself and your perspective about animals, death, grief, spirituality, and other topics explored in the series.

You'll also be invited to create what I call a "sacred story"—or, more accurately, a series of stories—about your life as an animal lover, pet keeper, animal advocate, environmentalist, or however you might describe yourself. A sacred story aims to answer some simple but challenging questions: What is your authentic identity as a human being amid all the diverse life-forms on this incredible planet? How have your personal interactions with animals and the natural world shaped your identity? And how can you lead a life in relationship with animals and the natural world that is spiritually directed and in keeping with your values? If such questions are important to you, then you're in the right place.

This kind of contemplative practice is essential in this age of rapid technological, cultural, and environmental change. Amid these vast shifts, many people are adopting new perspectives about the greater-than-human world. The spiritual landscape in the modern West is also changing. Among those who participate in a mainstream faith community, many approach their spiritual lives from a position of searching and questioning. Many people have left mainstream faith communities and are creating spiritual amalgamations that blend scientific understandings of the cosmos with traditional faith traditions and ancient spiritual practices. Still others contemplate the world through a values-based or humanist lens. Wherever you place yourself in this evolving spiritual landscape, the learning series will help you better understand the origins of your values and beliefs about animals and your spirituality.

You can read these books for personal interest or to support your healing journey, whether you're anticipating the imminent loss of a pet, actively grieving for a pet, or thinking about a pet lost years ago. The series' learning resources also make it a great fit for book study groups, and I encourage you to seek out others with whom you can share this journey of learning, healing, and spiritual growth. Your group might include your family and friends, coworkers, fellow church members in your place of worship, animal lovers you know through social media groups, or even people you meet at the dog park. Sharing your stories about animals and receiving others' stories with compassion will broaden your perspective on the human-animal bond and expand your ability to appreciate the diverse ways people think about and interact with animals.

The learning series is the culmination of thirty years of study, personal contemplation, spiritual care practice, and creative collaboration with pet keepers, animal advocates, environmentalists, and spiritual seekers. As noted earlier, I'll serve as your narrator and guide throughout the series, but it's important to note that my coauthor Karen has supported me throughout the development process. A talented writer and artist, Karen has helped me condense, organize, and synthesize years of practical insights and scholarship, and she's also contributed her own research to the wealth of scholarship cited in these books. Karen was also the lead writer for the series, so her voice is on every page, even when I appear to be doing all the talking.

Thank you for your interest in the Pet Chaplain Learning Series. Karen and I are delighted and humbled by the opportunity to share all we've learned with you. We hope you enjoy this learning experience and that, wherever your path may take you, you'll have a richer understanding of why animals are such an important part of our lives.

With gratitude—
Rob Gierka, EdD, and Karen Duke

Introduction

Many people take pride in their ability to shape their animal companions to exacting standards of conformity and dutiful behavior. Yet we don't often acknowledge the profound ways that our animals shape us.

The stories in this book demonstrate that our animal companions have a powerful impact on our lives. They teach us important lessons about loyalty, friendship, and nonjudgmental love. They draw us more fully into the present, allowing us to forget our cares and enjoy simply being alive. Their routines are our routines. Their lives are intertwined with ours, and when we lose them, we may feel as if a gaping hole has opened in our hearts and our homes.

This book is titled *Heart Animals* because it's packed with stories about animals who touch our hearts and change our lives. I gathered these stories while working on a doctoral research study of the human-animal bond and bereavement. As part of that study, I conducted one-on-one conversations with a small group of students enrolled in a two-year certification program in veterinary technology. In the US, veterinary professionals who complete this rigorous training are referred to as "vet techs," but in Europe they're called veterinary nurses, a title I believe more accurately reflects the nurturing, hands-on care they provide.

Although the conversations I had with the students were academic in purpose, these animal lovers and healers shared many of their most private and painful experiences with me, and I'm deeply grateful to them for taking me into their confidence. In hindsight, I can honestly say that I learned more about pet keeping and loss by talking with these aspiring veterinary professionals than I did in all my academic studies on the topic.

All the students I spoke with felt a strong connection with animals from their earliest memories, and they'd kept many pets throughout their lives. Yet they were all able to identify one or two pets who were especially important to them. We love all our animals. But if we're lucky, we might welcome a very special animal into our lives—a pet with whom we enjoy a particularly strong bond. These are our *heart animals*, a term that implies an extraordinary connection.

Our heart animals come into our lives in different ways. Maybe you enjoyed an inexplicable, instant connection with an animal, as if you were two old souls who were destined to find each other. Or maybe your heart animal was different somehow—more intuitive, playful, and attuned to your personality—than other animals you've known. Sometimes our heart animals are special to us because they're with us for so long, sharing our joys and sorrows and weathering life's ups and downs with steadfast loyalty and devotion. Regardless of how the bond develops, if you're lucky enough to have a heart animal in your life, you're likely to enjoy a tighter bond, a deeper connection, and a love that's stronger than any you've ever known. This kind of connection is rare, and it must be experienced to be truly appreciated. It's akin to the awe and wonder we enjoy when we're immersed in the beauty of the natural world, listen to great music, contemplate great works of art and literature, or share rituals, prayers, and songs in a place of worship. In a word, these relationships are *spiritual.*

The beauty of the relationships we enjoy with our heart animals is readily apparent in the stories the vet tech students shared with me. These rich oral histories trace the arc of their lives with their heart animals, from the moment these pets were welcomed into their homes to years of joyful companionship, the varied circumstances of the pets' death or loss, and the students' lives in the days, months, and years following the loss of their animals. The stories demonstrate years of love and companionship, the intense grief that comes with the loss of great love, and the wisdom and sense of identity and purpose the vet tech students gained through those experiences. On average, it had been nine years since these aspiring veterinary professionals had lost the pets they described in their conversations with me. Many still found it painful to revisit the circumstances of their pets' death, yet their memories were also filled with joy and gratitude.

The stories also speak to what calls to us. By *call*, I mean our life's calling. For the students I spoke with, their work in veterinary medicine was far more than a way to make a living. It was, I discovered, an ongoing expression of the enduring love they felt for the heart animals they'd lost and their desire to honor their pets' memories through their work. Their work was also an expression of their authentic identities as animal lovers and healers. When framed in this way, the tales you'll read in this book are all heroes' journeys—full of hardship, heartache, and sometimes tragedy but also full of love, joy, and hope.

I refer to such narratives as *sacred stories* because they reveal our deeply held values and our guiding purpose. Our sacred stories define who we are and what we value. They also connect us with others. When people receive our stories with love and compassion, we feel affirmed in who we are, and the things that lend our lives meaning and purpose feel good and right. If we're unable to share our sacred stories with the people in our lives, we may feel lost, adrift in a world that seems cold and indifferent to our greatest joys, deepest sorrows, and most profound meanings.

Sadly, people who love animals struggle to find others who hear them. My mission as a veterinary chaplain is to liberate people's sacred stories about their beloved animal friends. As a chaplaincy educator, I also want to empower people like you to be skilled story listeners. The more we can listen to each other's stories with patience, sympathy, and compassion, the better we can heal from our losses.

As the first book in the learning series, *Heart Animals* sets the stage for a journey of self-discovery and spiritual growth for people who love animals. In the next two books in the series—*Always in My Heart* and *Just an Animal*—you'll gain insight into how your heart animals have shaped your life, values, and spiritual identity. You'll explore the unique qualities of the human-animal bond, the hardships of saying goodbye to the animals who are an important part of our daily lives, and the powerful impact of our social experiences on how we perceive animals and ourselves in relationship with the greater-than-human world. A core part of this journey is what I call the "sacred story project." Each book in the learning series includes an installment of the sacred story project, and we'll begin this creative work in this volume.

I recommend saving the stories and reflections you compose as well as your responses to the discussion questions in an electronic format. You might also wish to keep a journal in which you jot down the thoughts, feelings, and insights that occur to you as you read the stories and other content presented in the series. You can refer to your journal when you engage with the discussion questions and work on your sacred story. Documenting your work will also give you a snapshot of where you are at this moment in your life, so if you revisit what you create now later on, you might be surprised at the insights you gained and how you've changed.

I also encourage you to set aside a regular time for reading and contemplation. Sometimes our greatest insights arise when we least expect it, as if our minds are continuously engaging in a quest for knowledge even when we're busy with our routine activities. For me, my greatest insights occur when I first wake up in the morning or when I'm walking in the woods. My coauthor, Karen, tells me she experiences her greatest "aha" moments while working in her garden. Find what works for you and cultivate a regular practice of self-reflection and contemplation as you undertake your spiritual journey.

Finally, be sure to practice good self-care when engaging with this book and subsequent books in the series. The discussion questions and the sacred story project will sometimes ask you to call forth memories of loved ones you've lost and carefully examine your feelings, including those that are uncomfortable or painful. Like most people, you've probably had quite a few upsetting experiences you've never thought about and grief you've pushed aside. Many of us are burdened by a tangle of unexamined grief, anger, regret, and guilt. Left to simmer, such unexamined feelings often surface in unexpected ways, which can be harmful to ourselves and others.

Thankfully, life is not all about distressing or painful emotions. When answering the discussion questions and writing your sacred story, be sure to also reflect on the ideas, people, and interactions that are filled with love and bring you joy. What do they have in common, and why do they make you feel happy? What life-giving lessons did you learn from the important people, animals, and sacred places in your life? And how have your spiritual experiences filled you with love and hope?

Be gentle with yourself on this journey. Cry or rage when you need to, allow yourself to feel your feelings, keep a journal and jot down whatever arises for you, and practice good self-care by getting plenty of rest, eating healthfully, and exercising. If you're feeling upset, take a walk, listen to your favorite music, engage in a relaxing hobby, write in your journal, pray, or meditate—whatever works for you. Above all, I encourage you to reach out to supportive family, friends, or a professional caregiver when you need to share your thoughts and feelings during this process.

No matter who you are or why you've picked up this book, I hope the stories and insights presented here and the other volumes in the Pet Chaplain Learning Series will strengthen your connection with your animal companions, past and present. Our pets shape us when they're with us. Yet even in death, they continue to teach us. Our love for our pets never dies but remains a rich resource within—a deep wellspring we can draw upon as we move forward in life. I believe this love—when we examine, sustain, and nurture it—can heal our hearts as we strive to make this world a better place for animals and the people who love them.

Sacred Stories

CHAPTER 1

Extraordinary Connections

I've been a veterinary chaplain for more than two decades, and over the years I've heard countless stories about animals—stories about dogs who behave like cats, cats who behave like dogs, turtles who come when called, pigs who like to play fetch, and birds who tease and tell jokes. I've heard inspiring stories about animals who saved their human guardian's life and others about pets whose loving presence helped someone weather a divorce, the death of a spouse or other family member, a job loss, or some other hardship. Ask someone to tell a story about a pet they've loved and lost, and their eyes will light up, even as tears stream down their face. And if you listen with curiosity and compassion to someone's story about their cherished animal, you may be privileged to step into their inner sanctum and gain insight into their greatest joys, deepest fears, abiding regrets, and highest hopes. I call this phenomenon the "pet portal" because I've discovered that our pets are like secret doorways that open directly into our hearts' most tender, vulnerable spaces.

In the coming chapters, we'll enter the pet portal and step into the inner worlds of ten people who are passionate about animals and have dedicated their lives to protecting and healing them. We'll gain insight into their profound sense of connection with animals, the social struggles that sometimes made it difficult for them to navigate their grief when their heart animals were lost, their determination to learn more so they could do more to help sick and injured animals, and their desire to ease the sorrow of people, like themselves, who love animals and grieve their loss. I'm deeply grateful to these students for having the courage to share their stories with honesty and authenticity.

As previously noted, I was conducting doctoral research on the human-animal bond and bereavement when I spoke with the students. I wanted to understand how their lives and, in particular, their interest in veterinary medicine had been influenced by their animal companions. I asked them to talk about those animals with whom they had a "special relationship." The only requirements were that these pets were not kept solely for utilitarian purposes, such as hunting or guarding, and they had died or otherwise been lost at least one year prior to the interview. I made the latter provision because I know it can take many years to fully appreciate the impact our animals have on our lives.

The interviews were semi-structured, meaning that I asked four primary questions. First, what was the nature of the bond the student had with their pet, both during the pet's life and after the pet's death? Second, what activities did they engage in to cope with the loss of their pet? Third, what were their social interactions relative to their pet during the pet's life and following the loss? And fourth, was there a connection between their relationship with their pet and their interest in veterinary medicine? In other words, was the student's career choice related to their pet in any meaningful way, either as a means of coping with the loss or honoring their pet's memory, or both? These were the basic touchpoints of the interviews, but my conversations with the students often diverged in unexpected directions.

The names of the students, their animals, and other personal details have been changed to protect the students' privacy, and the transcripts have been edited for ease of reading and narrative flow. Yet I've tried to preserve the unique voices of these animal caregivers, and after a brief introduction in which I share my impressions of the students, the stories appear in their own words.

The storytellers were a diverse group. Some grew up in the suburbs and others in rural areas. Some came from families that kept many pets, while others struggled to find acceptance from family members who viewed animals not as loved ones but as possessions. Regardless of their differences, however, all the students were passionate about animals and determined to give them a good quality of life. Many were involved in animal rescue, and all kept pets to whom they were devoted.

The career they'd chosen isn't for the squeamish or faint of heart. As you may know, a vet tech is most likely the person who greets you and your pet when you walk in the door of your veterinary clinic. They're the efficient, caring healers in scrubs who assist veterinarians in medical procedures, comfort ill and injured animals, calm those who are restive or aggressive, monitor and clean up after the animals kept at the clinic, and care for the bodies of those who've died. If you've ever received a difficult diagnosis for your pet or tearfully said your final goodbyes at your veterinary clinic, it may well have been a vet tech who comforted you. It's a tough job—one that's physically, mentally, emotionally, and spiritually demanding. My admiration for people who work in the veterinary profession and animal rescue increased exponentially after getting to know these remarkable people.

Out of sensitivity to my readers—especially those who are actively grieving for a pet—I'd like to offer the caution that some of the animals described in these stories died violently, and the descriptions of their deaths may be difficult to read. Yet I believe it honors each animal to depict their story as realistically as possible, even when those stories are agonizing. To fully grasp something, you must first name it. Tragedy? Yes, at times. Pain and suffering? Absolutely. Yet each storyteller became stronger and more resilient through their experiences with their heart animals and wiser through the telling of their stories. In the final analysis, these tales are love stories of the highest order.

Although these stories concern death and loss, they also show what's possible when we're able to navigate our grief with persistence and creativity. Each of the storytellers traced their interest in veterinary medicine to their heart animals. They all found a way to pay the love forward—to remember the love they felt for their pets and bring that love to their life's work. Some were motivated by a desire to correct past wrongs and give to others what they didn't receive when they lost their animals. Others were determined to share their positive experiences with the animals and pet keepers they served.

I encourage you to take your time reading these stories. There's a lot to unpack in each of them. If you keep pets, I expect you'll discover many kindred spirits as you recall your own heart animals and the gifts they brought to you. As you read, pay attention to the thoughts, feelings, and physical sensations that arise for you. Which stories make you feel happy? Which ones make you feel sad or angry? And which stories hit you especially hard? Reading mindfully may offer surprising insights into the stories and your own emotional life, values, and beliefs.

For those of you who are animal healers, protectors, or caregivers, I hope you'll be inspired to revisit your own experiences with your heart animals and consider the influence they may have had on your decision to pursue animal caregiving. Self-reflection will deepen your understanding of why you've chosen this path and strengthen your resolve to continue engaging in this challenging but rewarding work.

Gathering the stories presented in the next ten chapters was one of the most enriching experiences of my life. I remember rushing home after each interview, excited to share the amazing story I'd just heard with my life partner and coauthor Karen. We both fell in love with the stories and the storytellers. We felt humbled by the hard-won wisdom they had gained through their interactions with their heart animals. We were determined to honor the storytellers and their animals by sharing their tales with as many people as possible. We hope you enjoy getting to know them as much as we did.

CHAPTER 2

John and Dare

Dare was my friend. I had someone I could rely on.
She didn't judge me. She loved me no matter what,
and I loved her right back.

— John

I'd arranged to meet John in the library of the college where he attended classes, but something about the guy standing outside the library doors gave me pause. He was of medium height and solidly built with muscular forearms, bushy auburn hair, and a full beard, and he looked to be in his mid-forties—a demographic more in keeping with faculty than students. In his worn jeans and flannel shirt, leaning against the wall with one leg cocked and a boot pressed flat against the brick, he had a rock-and-roll coolness about him that roused my curiosity. I introduced myself and told him I was there to interview a student named John M—.

"Well, that would be me!" he said with a booming laugh. His handshake was warm and firm, his voice a gravelly baritone.

Together, we headed to a small meeting room in the library, where we settled into thinly padded gray chairs under the glare of fluorescent lights. John drummed his fingers on the table and hummed softly as I set up my tape recorder, shuffled papers, and plodded through the legalistic opening script required by my dissertation protocol.

Then we talked about his pets, his family, his childhood, life and death, and life after death. John had always loved animals and laughed a lot as he reminisced about all the animals he'd kept over the years. As a kid, he used to capture house spiders, though he always let them go after studying them a bit. He later bought a tarantula, who he named after Gene Simmons of the rock band Kiss. "Unfortunately, I didn't have Gene for very long before he died," John said. "So I put him in a shoe box, buried him in the backyard, gave him his respects, you know. He was a cool little guy."

Then there was Mick the iguana, named after Mick Jagger. "I kept Mick for about three or four years," John recalled. "But bad luck struck, and I wound up being homeless. I'd built him this huge terrarium, and I put it in a storage shed. I kept all the heating pad lights on and checked on him every week, but then one winter night the storage company shut the power off, and he froze to death."

John also reminisced about his favorite cat, who he named after Jimmy Page of Led Zeppelin. "I took Jimmy to the lake when he was just a little kitten," John said, smiling at the memory. "At first, he'd just dig his claws into me and ride along when I went swimming, and it hurt like hell. But after a while, he'd swim right beside me. He loved going to the lake. That cat loved to swim."

Mostly John talked about his childhood dog Dare. His story provides insight into the one quality most pet keepers mention when asked what they value most about their pet: unconditional love. In John's case, Dare loved him when he struggled to find acceptance among his family and friends as a youth, and it was Dare's steadfast, joyful presence that helped John survive a childhood that he described as a struggle. As he spoke of his youth, I was struck by the connection he drew between his vivid memories of the verdant landscape of his childhood home and his memories of Dare. As Czech writer Milan Kundera observed, "Dogs are our link to paradise. They don't know evil or jealousy or discontent. To sit with a dog on a hillside on a glorious afternoon is to be back in Eden, where doing nothing was not boring—it was peace."[1]

John

I got Dare when I was about nine or ten years old. Her full name was Darrelly, which is a combination of my mom and dad's middle names and my middle name, but we always just called her Dare. It was my mom who came up with the name because my grandmother had a dog that was named Jarelee, which was my first cousin's and my middle name abbreviated and put together. I guess using our names for our pets was my family's way of really connecting the animals with the family.

The animal thing runs in my family. My aunt, uncle, and three cousins had a hoard of cats at any given time. And even though my aunt was allergic to cats, she'd sit on the front steps of her house and check all those cats for ticks and fleas and do what needed to be done. When I was a teenager, I lived with my aunt and uncle for a few years. They were my favorite relatives. I'd sit down and help my aunt with the cats because I felt so bad for her. Her eyes would get red and puffy, and she would be sneezing, but she would stick right there and clean them, preen them, and make sure they were good. No cuts or sores. If they did need anything, if it was just a cut or something, she'd fix it herself because she was a nurse. Everybody helped everybody else in that household—person, animal, or whatnot. The dogs would nurse the cats sometimes if the mother rejected the kittens. There was one dog who would nurse kittens and play mother to them. It was great.

My family had always had cats, and then my parents started talking about getting a dog. They brought Dare home one day, though they never really knew what kind of mix she was. She may have had some Jack Russell in her because she was a small dog. She had a long, sharp nose and a brown-and-white coat, and her ears flopped over a little bit. Now, I won't lie, but when I first saw her, I was like, "Oh, man, I don't want this dog." I was just a kid, and I think I was expecting something like a German shepherd, and then I got this little mutt. But just by interacting with her and getting to know her personality, I really came to love that dog.

When I was a kid, my daily life was a struggle. I didn't have very many good days. Most every day, I was getting picked on or into fights. We were poor, or at least I thought I was poor. My parents might have had money, but I sure didn't. And I was just different. Looking back, I can see that some of the kids I knew in school were mean as hell. They'd gather around me, five or six kids at a time, wanting to fight. I'd ask them to stop, but most of the time, when it came down to it, we'd be scrapping. Then what made it worse was that my teachers didn't believe that I didn't start the fights. My parents didn't believe me. I was always the troublemaker, no matter what. My grandmother was the only one who believed me. From what I understand, she actually went up to the school and confronted them about blaming me all the time. But it didn't do much good. I ended up getting into even more fights after that.

So yeah, I'd come home from another bad day at school, and Dare would be sitting on the front step. I'd sit with her, and she'd put her nose in my lap and nudge my hand, flip it up, and get me to pet her. She'd roll over on her back and let me rub her belly. She loved that. And I'd start petting her, and it seemed like whatever was going on just wasn't that bad. The way she'd look, the way she'd tilt her head to the side, those eyes would reflect how I was feeling, just like she knew. It always took the edge off my mood. She knew I was hurting, and petting her, walking her, would help me out. I'd pet her until a lot of the pain subsided. Then I'd play ball with her. That helped get that bad energy out of me, just throwing the ball, chasing her around, or walking her.

Dare was really energetic and always happy. She loved an open field. I miss watching her run through those fields where the grass was taller than she was, and her leaping above it where you could see her for just a moment. She looked like a deer. She'd fold her front legs and hop just like a deer. She could clear a four-foot fence without a problem. It was a nightmare keeping her in the backyard.

I'd walk her and feed her every day, and I'd take her everywhere with me when I could. We'd wander the train tracks. Other times we'd walk into town and just sit and watch people play baseball or football. If there was broken glass, I'd pick it up because I didn't want her walking through that. I tried to teach her to walk alongside my bicycle, but she didn't take to that real good. When she got tired, she wouldn't give me a warning. She'd just lie down and—poof—I'm off the bike. I tried that twice. The second time she pulled me off the bike, I bandaged up my knees and elbows and said, "OK, we're just walking." So we mostly walked.

We lived out in the country, and a lot of times, Dare and I would go down to the swamp. I'll never forget the first time we went there. It stunk so bad, but she was determined to go down in there, so I put up with it. Then after a while, I didn't care. It was like, "All right. We're going looking for something, whatever she's got her nose scented to." If she smelled something, she'd take off after it. Sometimes it'd be a lizard. Sometimes it'd be something that just started off in the woods, and she got it in her head to go after it. I was right behind her. It worked out great. She'd find all the critters, and I'd catch them—snakes, lizards, toads, stuff like that. And then my mama would get mad at both of us for coming home all nasty from running around in the swamp and bringing along these weird critters.

Dare was just always there, always steady. I can't say she ever pulled me out of a burning building or saved me from drowning or anything super spectacular. But she was just loving, and she was there at a time in my life when I really needed her. She was a constant companion, kind of an anchor for me. She was my friend. I had someone I could rely on. She didn't judge me. She didn't blame me for my clothes being torn or me being all beat up or hearing this other kid was in the hospital because we got into a fight. She loved me no matter what, and I loved her right back.

And that's the bond I've had with animals. They don't judge you. They're there for you. They just want to be treated right and loved, and they'll give that love right back. She was the first dog I ever had that kind of bond with. To me, if the companionship is right, you can have the same bond with every animal. My dog now, I love him to death. But he's not my first dog. So yeah, I think Dare was extra special. Having to walk her at such a young age, clean up after her—she helped teach me responsibility, how to properly care for another living thing. And I had someone to love at a time when I really needed it the most.

Dare and I had a good life together for close to ten years. I'd already moved away from home when my parents decided to have her euthanized. I remember being upset about it. I got that pit in my stomach and felt like my heart was dragging. I was mad too. I was thinking, "They're killing my dog." I wanted my dog to live, and I thought there had to be something that medicine could do. But, you know, you get older, the body breaks down, and eventually you go. Fortunately, that's what happened to her. It wasn't a car accident. It wasn't mistreatment. It wasn't being poisoned by a neighbor or any of these other horror stories you hear. Dare had a nice, healthy, comfortable life, and she grew old and passed.

But I was just a kid when she was euthanized, maybe eighteen years old—thought I knew everything, didn't know nothing. I didn't accept her death at first. But after I thought about it some more, I knew it was the best thing my folks could have done for her at the time. Because at the end, she was really suffering. She had mange and arthritis and was getting to the point where she couldn't walk anymore. And she was missing so many teeth that she could barely eat. It hurt me when she died, but it was for the best. Her suffering was over.

We wound up burying her in the backyard—had a little service, said a few words for her, and let her go on her way. I remember that after the funeral, I had a sense of relief because I knew she was in a better place. She was happy again.

I was raised going to church. I don't buy into a lot of it, but I always liked the images of peace it brought me. My parents, a lot of my family, are really big into their religion, and a lot of the time that's the way I'd hear it phrased—you know, the deceased is with family and friends. In Dare's case, she's a dog. She got what her heart's desire was in heaven. I see her running through fields, hunting, doing what dogs love to do. It's a nice vision to have, so I more or less choose to see it that way, that she's at peace doing what she wants to do and waiting for the rest of us to show up.

To be honest, I don't think about Dare all that often anymore. It's been a long time since she died. But every now and then, when I see a dog that looks like her, I'll get a picture in my mind of her running and digging and doing all the stuff she loved to do. When I think back, I can picture Dare just like we were, playing ball together or walking down those old roads. In fact, sometimes that's the only time I can really remember my hometown is when I think of her. For some people, music triggers them and gets them to remember certain events and times and places. Sometimes it's the smell of something cooking. With me, it's always been my pets that take me back.

So Dare helped me out, you know? And I think that's one of the reasons I enjoy helping out animals. Because I'm the kind of guy, if I'm going down the freeway doing a hundred and ten, and I see a turtle, I'll block all the traffic and move that turtle. Now, don't get me wrong. I'll help out people too. I'll give you the shirt off my back if I can. But I've never been hurt by helping an animal. Animals don't take advantage of you. They don't look at you like you're weak for helping them out, and they don't expect anything in return. I think, all in all, that's one of the reasons I relate to animals better than to people.

I think a large part of my decision to become a vet tech is the fact that animals never judge you. The hurt I've had from people was worse than the hurt I've had from animals on their worst day. I've been bitten, scratched, and bruised by a terrified one-hundred-pound dog. But animals aren't acting out to be hateful, mean, or spiteful, and there's nothing like the genuine joy you see from these animals when they feel better. They may come into the clinic snappy and irritable and foul. But when they're feeling better and they're back to being right, it's great. There aren't many things on this planet that express joy to me like animals do when they know you've helped them out.

CHAPTER 3

Kelly, Daisy, and Zuzu

There's something about looking a dog in the eye.
I truly believe that a dog can see inside your soul
and see what kind of person you are.

— Kelly

Kelly was in her early twenties, a small woman, always in motion. When she spoke, she talked with her whole body, her hands waving to punctuate her stories and her right foot bouncing slightly. She had a strong presence and seemed remarkably comfortable in her own skin. I came to learn that this young woman had found her element—her way of being powerful in the world—by helping animals and the people who love them. Kelly was on a mission.

Kelly said she loved animals in a "freakish way." She seemed to consider herself something of an oddball because of her intense love of animals. "I Zoom with my dog Magpie," she said. "I'm one of those, OK? I know it sounds really weird, but I love animals more than I love people because animals will show you love even if you don't have love anywhere else."

Kelly had already spent years working as a veterinary assistant, beginning with an internship in high school. She talked passionately about her work's challenges and rewards, sharing insights into a difficult job that requires doing things to animals you don't want to do, things that sometimes hurt them. Even though she saw a lot of suffering and death every day, she loved her work.

One thing that struck me about Kelly's story was her keen sensitivity to the physical presence of animals. She appeared to have a gift for communicating with animals through her body and her eyes. In the words of philosopher Martin Buber, "An animal's eyes have the power to speak a great language."[1] Kelly was fluent in the language of animals. Her connection with her hamster Daisy, her dog Zuzu, and all her other pets appeared to be both physical and spiritual. For Kelly, the simple act of looking into a dog's eyes—and the wordless exchange that can occur when you really see an animal and they see you—was a deeply spiritual experience.

Kelly

I've had all sorts of animals. I've had birds, hermit crabs, hamsters, rats, dogs, cats, snakes, and everything else. My mom even had a monkey at one point. We had them all. It sounds funny to me now, but one of the pets I decided to talk to you about was a hamster. Her name was Daisy, and I got her when I was five. She lived for almost five years, which is absurdly long for a hamster. Most hamsters only live about a year and a half, maybe two. At that time, I lived with my mom, dad, sister, and brother. We lived overseas because my dad was in the military. We had two Rottweilers—Zuzu and Lady. And I had Daisy. She was my best friend.

Things didn't go well in my family, and my parents ended up divorcing when I was seven. After the divorce, my mom moved my sister, brother, and me back to the US while my dad stayed overseas. It was easy enough to bring the dogs along, but it wasn't easy to move

Daisy because we had to go to Hawaii to get back to the States from where we were living overseas, and hamsters are illegal in Hawaii. My mom told me that before we made the trip, she tried to find a hamster identical to Daisy in the US, but couldn't because Daisy was so big, and female hamsters are hard to find there to begin with. She paid $600 to have Daisy flown back to the US. The funny thing is, Daisy had to have a military escort to fly through Hawaii. She was put in a rat cage inside a bird cage inside a cat carrier inside a small dog kennel inside a large-breed kennel, escorted by three huge guys in military uniforms. It's funny when you think about it. All that for one little hamster.

We hadn't been back in the States long when my mom moved Daisy and me out West. My sister and brother went to live with their dad because they had a different dad than I did, and everyone else in my family lived on the East Coast. My mom and I moved a lot, and Daisy was with me through the first four homes we lived in out West. My mom worked long hours, and I was going through some stuff that I shouldn't have been going through. And my mom is not the nicest woman. I love my mom, but she's not a motherly, nurturing person. At that time, Daisy was my everything. She was my best friend, my sister, and my brother. She was the only thing I really had. I talked to her all the time. She would snuggle in my bed with me, sitting right here over my heart, or she would sit on my shoulder when I walked around the house. She was mine. No one could take her away from me, and with everything else going on with my family, that meant a lot.

We bred Daisy at one point and had twenty-eight hamsters, and that was just craziness. We're not hamster people, and it was random that I got a hamster and fell in love with her because I haven't had a hamster since. But like I said, at that time in my life, she was super important to me. She was really calm, maybe because she was so fat. She was huge. She was probably the size of a guinea pig. I'm sure she died of a heart attack from overfeeding, to be honest with you. I used to feed that hamster way too much food. Goodness gracious.

One day after school, my mom sat me down and told me that

Daisy had passed. Her death really upset me. But there were a lot of unspoken rules in my family, and one of those was about dealing with loss. You're allowed to be sad for a little while, and then you move on. My dad's favorite line was, "Just deal with it." By the time Daisy died, I had lost my dad, sister, brother, and grandparents. They didn't die, but they weren't a part of my life. After you lose so much, you can't get so emotional about things. I remember crying and being upset for a couple of days when Daisy died, and then I went back to being normal.

Still, it was nice that we buried her. We froze her because we didn't know where we wanted to bury her at first. We eventually buried her on the side of a mountain where they were doing construction. My mom's boyfriend at the time was working on the construction site, and he buried her there for me. We put her in a shoebox and talked about her. Just us. I guess it was a memorial in a way. We talked about her, what she meant to us, and how we loved her.

When I think about Daisy now, I feel warm, like there's still something there. I feel like she's still a part of me, even though she's not here. She still holds a special place in my heart because I get a warm ache in my chest when I think about her. I guess I'd describe it as joy. I feel happy when I think about Daisy. That time I had with her was so important. The memories make me smile, and I sometimes think, "Oh, yeah, I had that once." I had unconditional love from somebody when I really needed it, and I know if I hadn't had that, I probably wouldn't have made it as far as I did in my younger years. I probably wouldn't have come out on the other side. Daisy helped me through a lot. She made me realize how much animals can do for you. I feel so thankful when I think of her.

• • •

The other pet who was special to me was Zuzu, one of our Rottweilers. We had her for fourteen years. My mom had her before I was born. She died when I was seven, right after we came back to the US from overseas. She died before Daisy did, when my brother and sister were still living with us.

Zuzu was the best dog you could ever imagine. She was like my mama. She treated me like a puppy. She used to sleep in my bed when I was a baby. She'd sleep in the crib. That dog—I was her baby for sure, because I was less than a year old when she had her first litter, and we gave her puppies away, so I think she adopted me. I used to cuddle with her on the ground, and I'd crawl on top of her and ride on her back. She taught me how to walk. She used to lie down on the ground next to me, and I would grab onto her. She'd stand halfway up and army crawl on the ground and walk me along. We have videos of it. It's hilarious. She used to carry my easter basket around for me, and I'd pick up eggs.

My mom tells a story about how we used to feed the rotties these big bones from the butcher. Well, Zuzu had this bone, and I wanted to play with it. I was a toddler at the time. She was gnawing on it and went to eat it, but I wouldn't let go. My mom said she walked into the kitchen, and my arm was all the way down the dog's mouth, in her throat with this bone, and she was sitting there with her mouth open, frozen, because she didn't want to bite me. My mom freaked out. She pulled my arm out along with the bone because I still wouldn't let go. Zuzu never bit me. She was such a good dog.

I remember when Zuzu passed. It was hard for me. I remember curling up in a ball behind the front door where Zuzu would lie and crying and crying, lying there by the door. My mom tried to move me, but I refused, and eventually I fell asleep. My mom picked me up and took me to the rocking chair, where I curled up in a little ball again and cried some more. My sister and brother were really supportive because they could see how upset I was, and they were upset too.

We had Zuzu cremated. She's been gone about fifteen years now, but she's still in my mother's home. Her ashes are in an urn with this cute little statue of her on top, and it sits on the bottom stair facing the front door. Whenever I go back to my mom's house and walk in the door, I see her sitting there. And if it's been a really tough day, I'll stop and talk to her, like, "Hi, Zuzu. How are you? I wish you were still here. I miss you." I still think of her as my guardian angel, and part of me thinks she's up there watching me.

• • •

When I was four years old, maybe five, my mom and I were driving somewhere, and my mom goes, "Kelly, what do you want to be when you grow up?"

And I said I want to be a "peterinarian."

And she goes, "Don't you mean veterinarian?"

"No, I want to be a peterinarian."

"Well, what's the difference between a veterinarian and a peterinarian?"

"I want to take care of the animals that need love."

And since that day, that's all I wanted to do. I wanted to take care of animals. I've always had a huge soft spot for them—I mean, freakishly huge. I'm not a veterinarian, at least not yet. Maybe someday I will be.

I think my pets brought me to this work: Daisy, Zuzu, Magpie, Stormy, Chip, Sundrop, Spencer, Lady, Barnaby, and all the other animals I've had. All those relationships have taught me that there are people for whom pets are just pets, and those people make me angry because sometimes they don't take care of the animals the way they should. And then there are those people who need extra love and compassion because their animals are family. I understand what that means, and because I can relate to that, I can help people when their animals are sick. I can tell them that I know how much they love their pet, and these are your options, and we'll do everything in our power to save them. Because animals have played such a huge role in who I am mentally and physically, I feel I'm a good person for this job.

In my opinion, humans are easy. They're a piece of cake. You tell them to sit and stay, and they'll sit and stay and hold their arm real still so the nurse can poke them with a big needle. You tell a dog to sit and stay and try to poke it with a big needle and see how well that works out for you, OK? I wish they would sit still and hold out their leg. Do you know how much easier that would make my job? But the reality is that you have to pin animals down, and I think it helps to look them in the eye. It's what I've always done. Because if you hold a dog down without looking at him, you don't even know who you are holding, and they'll spazz out and try to kick or bite you. But if you take the time to look at them and you go, "It's going to be OK," then everything goes more smoothly.

Not many people have the compassion or patience to work with animals. I've worked with people who won't even take the time to look at an animal. I mean, it doesn't take but ten seconds to do it. I get much more positive responses from animals than some people do because those ten extra seconds really make a difference. I've never been bitten by the animals I've worked with, and—knock on wood here—I've never had any serious issues. You have the dogs that are a hassle in the first place. But if you can look at them and give them that moment of comfort, it helps.

In a way, comforting an animal by making eye contact with them makes me feel better about all the things I have to do in my work. Because I'm not doing very nice things to these animals. This job can be tough, and it can get to people. It takes a lot of patience. Now, don't get me wrong. I have my days when I'm like, "I'm so over this. I want to go home. I'm sick of this." But then I think about Zuzu and everything she had to go through with the cancer, and I hope—I pray—that someone was there for her. I hope the doctor really did comfort my mom in the way she said he did, that there was that care, there was that love. To this day, I think about Zuzu sometimes and how scared she could have been in her situation, and I hope someone took the time to comfort her. That's one of the reasons I give extra care to someone else's pet—because I know that cat or dog is their family member.

I think about the bond I had with Daisy and Zuzu when I see other people with their pets. There's always someone in a family who has a stronger bond with the animal than anybody else. And it's hard to see those people lose an animal, especially when you go above and beyond and do everything you can to help the animal when they're sick or injured. But there's only so much you can do. It's tough. I've seen death a lot, and it sucks every time. I've "bagged and tagged" a lot of dogs. It sounds awful, but that's a saying for when animals die. They're double bagged in these giant black bags, and then you tag them with their name to send them to either the crematorium or wherever the owner wants them to go. The vet techs have to bag and tag the animals. I might get in trouble for saying this, but I've noticed that some people will toss the animal in the bag. Not in a mean way, but they're kind of like, "OK, here you go." Then they tie up the bag, and whatever.

But to this day, no matter how many times I do it, I take the time to avoid hurting the dog as I'm putting them in the bag. They're dead, but I still don't want to hurt them. My boss used to make fun of me because she's been doing it for forty years. But I don't care. I think of it this way: If it were my dog, I wouldn't want her thrown into a bag without any care. You know what I mean? Like, god, that sucks. That animal is someone's family member. Now, there are some crappy owners out there who don't care, and when I have crappy owners, I try to be extra compassionate and gentle with those animals. Because animals will give you unconditional love, and when they don't get it back, it's unfair. They continue to give it to you. I almost wish they'd stop giving so much love when they're not treated with love, but they can't. That's just how animals are.

There's something about looking a dog in the eye. I truly believe that a dog can see inside your soul and see what kind of person you are, and I truly believe that you have to have a good soul to work in this field. Otherwise, the animals will know. I know that's weird, and I feel like a freak for saying that, but that's what I believe, and that's what I've seen. I've noticed that people who take the time to show the animal who they are and make a connection get a much more positive response, and those people have a better heart and soul than the others. They're more caring, more nurturing. Animals are so much smarter than people give them credit for. They know what you're feeling, and they respond to your attitude. Now, I'm not super religious by any means, but I think that animals were placed here by a bigger force, whether it be God or whatever else, to comfort humans. If you take the time and energy to care and make a connection with an animal, they really are your heart and soul, and I think they really do guide us.

I learned the soul thing from Zuzu. She was a part of me. I can still remember her eyes, those big brown and gold eyes. I remember sitting on the ground as a kid, and she would sit with me. She would lay her head on my lap and look up at me. I'd talk to her about everything, and she would make me feel so soft and warm and free from everything. I remember knowing that she loved me.

Losing any pet is tough, but there are always those special ones that stick with you a little longer than the others. Every time I see a Rottweiler, I think of Zuzu. She's the first dog who comes to mind. Every time I see a brindle dog, I think of my dog Magpie, and every time I see a hamster, I think of Daisy. Whenever people say, "Oh, I had a hamster" or "My daughter's hamster . . ." or whatever, I always tell the story of Daisy. I always tell them I had a hamster for four and a half years once, and she was my best friend.

As I said, I'm not super religious, but I do pray sometimes, and every once in a while when I send up a prayer or say good night, I sometimes say, "Good night, Daisy." I feel dumb saying this, but when I was little, my mom and I used to have a bedtime prayer, and we would call out everyone in the family. I always started with Mommy and Daddy, then my sister and brother, and then Zuzu, Lady, and Daisy. My pets always came right after my immediate family but before Grandma and Grandpa and aunts and uncles and cousins.

I still love all my old pets, even the ones that I wasn't super attached to. I still love them like crazy. Whenever I talk about the pets I've lost, I talk about them as if they were still alive. Because in some ways they are. They're all still with me, in my heart.

CHAPTER 4

Frank and Muppet

We think we teach the animals, and we do.
But they teach us as well

— Frank

Frank arrived promptly at 2 p.m. for our interview in the same private meeting room of the college library where I met most of the vet tech students. Unlike most of the students, however, Frank was in his sixties. He was a small, wiry man with buzz-cut gray hair and sharp blue eyes, and he came to our interview dressed in green scrubs and tennis shoes.

I'd asked the students to bring pictures of their pets because photos are always a good way to kick off a conversation about an animal. While most of the students I spoke with had photos of their animals on their smartphones, Frank arrived with two huge photo albums. I later learned that Frank had enjoyed a long career in the military before retiring to pursue a second career in veterinary medicine, and those albums were packed with photos of his world travels.

"I have tens of thousands of pictures of animals from all over the world," he said. "Most people go to the hot spots when they travel—the tourist places, the shopping malls, you know. I'm just the opposite. I'll rent a car and get as far away from the norm as possible. Everywhere I've gone in the world—and I've been lucky enough to go quite a few places—I go see the animals."

I remember Frank flipping through one of the albums, smiling and telling stories about the photos, before stopping at a picture of a diminutive calico cat looking calmly at the camera with bright-green eyes. This was Muppet, who was Frank's constant companion for nearly a quarter century and had a profound influence on his beliefs about animals. Frank had grown up on a farm and said he was raised to regard animals more as "equipment" than loving companions. But over the years, Muppet taught him to look at animals differently—not as useful objects but as living beings deserving of a good quality of life.

Muppet was truly a change agent in Frank's life. He probably wouldn't have arrived at his moral framework regarding animals if he hadn't fallen in love with that beautiful calico. He also may never have pursued a second career as a vet tech if it weren't for Muppet. His work was her legacy, and her spirit continued to live on through the lives of all the animals he cared for.

Frank

Muppet was a cat I found. She'd been discarded from a litter of kittens as the runt. She was a calico, and her colors were just fantastic. She only had one little spot of white on her, and all the rest of her colors were creams, grays, and blacks, and she actually had blue in her coat. She was just amazing. I think that's probably one of the reasons why I thought to myself, "I'm going to keep you."

For the next twenty-two and a half years, that cat and I bonded. We were friends. We ate together, slept together—we did everything together, except when I worked or took a short vacation. We had experiences over a lifetime. The relationship was special, partly because we were together for so long. We even lived together in a vehicle at a time when things weren't going well. She moved with me from the East Coast to the West Coast to the Midwest, back to the West Coast and, ultimately, to the Rocky Mountains, which is where she passed away.

I have a lot of memories of her and the years we spent together—mostly good, some not so good. I almost killed her once. When she was five or six years old, we were living on the West Coast. My wife and I put her in the car because we were leaving to go to the mountains for about a month, and I wasn't going to leave her behind. We parked the car to go someplace, and I left her in the car with the windows cracked. I was only in the store about an hour, but that cat was soaked from ear to paws from sweating and panting. I mean just drenched. I'd always lived in colder climates, so I just didn't think there would be a problem, but we were in the desert. That was a defining moment in our lives.

She could be a bit of a stinker too. I spent a lot of time in Spain for my work, and I used to collect these porcelain figures called Lladrós. They're one-of-a-kind, handmade, absolutely beautiful figurines. I would buy them and ship them home to my mom for safekeeping because I was still traveling. One time I bought this particularly nice piece that I decided to keep with me, and I put it up on a shelf where there was no way an animal could get to it. And I'll be darned if Muppet didn't manage to break it. She jumped up there and pushed it off. And I swear to this day she thought that maybe I put that figurine a little bit above her in the pecking order, and she decided to break it. So I almost killed her once, and then I wanted to kill her! [laughing]

There are a few memories like that that stand out for me. But it was really her day-to-day presence that shaped our relationship. We were rarely apart. Every day she'd be there to greet me when I came home from work. Whether the wife was home, the dog was home, it didn't matter who was home—that cat was waiting for me at the door, just like a dog. She could tell if it was my car, even if I was blocks away, and she'd sit there waiting. And every day it was a chore to get from the front door to where I was going because she'd do this weaving thing between my feet. Finally, when I would settle in for the evening, she'd be right there, sitting on my lap while I read or watched TV. She slept with me for years, snuggled behind my knees, and then, for some reason, she decided it would be fun to climb up on the headboard and jump on me in the middle of the night, claws first. Well, that stopped her from sleeping in the bedroom, and at first it was like making a child sleep in their own bed.

It was a relationship like any other, but in some ways it was better. Even family members you have arguments with. Yet you love them regardless. Well, that same relationship without those arguments? Without those disappointments? Without those judgments? Without the heartbreak of their disappointments in life? It's pretty easy to maintain that kind of relationship.

· · ·

I've had animals all my life. I grew up on a farm, and we had horses, cattle, chickens, a sheepdog, you name it. I appreciated those animals not as pets but as equipment. It wasn't until later in life that I was able to experience animals as pets.

I always felt a bond with animals. Even when I went hunting as a kid, I felt a connection with what I was hunting. I feel the same thing with all animals, but the sense of connection was much deeper with Muppet, in part because I had her for such a long time. Spending that much time with an animal is definitely a learning experience.

I've had lots of litters of cats and dogs and farm animals too, like pigs and sheep. And for some reason, I was always interested in the runts of the litter. A lot of them do really well, but they don't tend to live as long as the others. I always took it as a personal goal to help the runts. As a child, I'd nurse them. I did the same thing with Muppet. I took care of her, from feeding her with an eyedropper when she was a tiny kitten to the time she passed away. It was an entire life of learning and watching. Because I had so much time one-on-one with her, I started noticing small changes in her, things about her movements. I paid attention to how she walked, how she lay down, how she jumped. After a while, I could tell when she wasn't eating right. I could look at her body, and I could almost sense if she had a gastric impaction because she wasn't drinking as much as she should when she was eating the dry food. And so, for a couple of days, I would supplement with canned food, or I'd wet her dry food so that she would get more water and move the impaction. Beyond that, I made an effort to make sure she had a good life with the best foods, appropriate exercise, regular vaccinations, and limiting her exposure to illness.

I believe that other animals deserve the same care. When you see an animal and notice they're uncomfortable, it doesn't matter whether they're your favorite pet or the gorilla at the zoo or the cow or the swine that's going to slaughter. While they're on this earth and as long as we're in possession of the animal, it's our responsibility to give them the best life possible. And that's a belief that came from my relationship with Muppet. Muppet made me feel better on bad days. An animal can make you feel wonderful. Animals have bad days too, and you can bring joy to their lives. The connection I hold on to is that there's always a two-way street. It's always a give and take. It's a learning experience. We think we teach the animals, and we do. But they teach us as well.

When I was growing up and taking care of animals, I had to feed them and water them, but I didn't appreciate the quality of their life at the time. Well, there's a difference between giving basic care and giving quality of life. You can care for a human or an animal and give them the basic necessities. Or you can take that same person or animal and give them understanding and love and a good quality of life, and I think you get all of that back. Muppet taught me that.

My decision to study veterinary technology as a second career stems in large part from the years I spent caring for Muppet. She lived to be almost twenty-three years old, so my ability to help her without having any experience or training worked out very well. I can't imagine what I could do for animals with a little education and some good work experience. The connection I had with animals all my life, and especially my connection with Muppet and my desire to give her the best life possible—not just comfort but health—taught me that I really enjoy doing that, and I've enjoyed that with all the animals I've had since Muppet.

I can help other people learn too. I think it's important to educate everyday people about their animals because there are a lot of people—clients, owners—who don't quite understand the relationship they have with their animal. Even adults don't fully understand the responsibility they're taking on when they go to the pet store, pick this animal up, and take it home. There's a whole lot more to true care than giving an animal food and water. And when people don't understand the relationship that needs to happen for everything to work well, animals end up in despair. But if you do provide the proper care, you're rewarded with a healthier animal and lower veterinary bills. You'll have a more well-behaved animal and a cleaner house, and you'll be rewarded with love and companionship. You know, the only bad animals are animals that haven't been trained correctly or shouldn't have been trained at all. You don't bring a lion cub into your home and raise him as a lion and not expect him to rip your arm off.

I'm an animal advocate because at some point in my life it really snapped in my head that these animals are totally helpless once we take them from their natural environment. I'm not ashamed that I'm a strong Christian, and I believe that God provides for what God has put on this earth. And if there's an animal on the wild side of the fence, God knows what that animal needs, and that animal will get what it needs. It will be provided for. But once you take that animal out of God's hands, and you take control? Then you need to take responsibility. And a lot of people don't do that.

• • •

The only drawback about pets is that they break your heart. They get old, they get sick, they get hurt. And they can't always tell you what's wrong. I found out that Muppet had died when I got a phone call. I can't say for sure how or why she died. She was very old for a cat—almost twenty-three—but she was in good health as far as I knew. My hunch is that she died of loneliness. People may not understand or believe it, but I think loneliness can play a huge role in our physical health. There are cases—and I've experienced it in my family—where two souls are together for many years, and suddenly one's gone, and the other one's will to continue living dies.

Muppet and I had not been separated since she was a baby. At nineteen or twenty years old, she started having some health issues, but it was all manageable with diet. Overall, she was a good, healthy cat. But then I took a new position that required me to be out of the country, and I was gone almost a year. And within six months of my leaving, I think Muppet just gave up on living. A family member who was taking care of her said that, within a few days of me being gone, her temperament changed, and her health started going downhill. And then she just went to sleep one night and didn't wake up the next day. I think her will to continue living left when I wasn't there anymore. She was used to having me there all the time: my smells, my touch, my voice, my humanness. I think that's probably how she died.

Muppet is buried out West, where I still have a house. That's where I grew up, and that's where I'm heading once I graduate. She's buried out in the forest with several other animals. A gentleman I used to work for owns fifteen acres out in the forest, and that's where some of our animals are buried together. Anybody who knew me knew that she had passed away. You don't have a pet for that long a time and lose it and not talk about it. Even people who probably didn't want to hear about Muppet's death heard about it anyway. Everyone responded appropriately, as I recall. No one said, "Oh, darn. Sorry. Try again." I felt like I had good support when she died—primarily from my mom and also the people I worked with. I'm thankful for that.

Losing Muppet was very hard. I guess you could say it was like losing a family member who's up there in years. You understand they led a full life and aren't suffering. But losing her—losing the material part of her—hit me hard. Muppet was a beautiful cat, very soft and very lovable. But her soul and her emotions and everything else about her have been with me all along, so I never really lost her.

It's the same with people who are very close. When they're separated, they can still feel the other person with them, not necessarily in a physical sense, and yet the mind can play tricks on you. You know that person isn't there, but you can still smell their perfume. Memories can create senses. I mean, I can still feel Muppet rub up against my leg. I can actually *feel* her. And if the cat I have now jumps up in my lap, I think of how Muppet would stretch out and wrap her limbs around my legs. There are a lot of things that spark those memories, those sensations. I constantly see her. I don't even have to close my eyes, and I can see her.

Even though Muppet is gone, she's still with me all the time in heart and spirit. She's just part of my life. And I can still feel the love. When you experience unconditional love, you never forget it, and, unfortunately, there are very few humans who can give unconditional love. An animal is born that way, and once you've experienced that, it's always with you. The unconditional love I had with Muppet continues to educate me and show me how to be open to other animals, how to try to give more. We're human, and we make mistakes. We judge people. Even the best people judge people. But having unconditional love like that for a long time made me start trying to do it myself.

CHAPTER 5

Mollie and Honey

I want to do for someone else what
couldn't be done for me.

— Mollie

Mollie came to our interview dressed in faded jeans, a concert T-shirt for a popular country music band, and scuffed cowboy boots. She was small but solidly built, and I suspected she was a dynamo whose diminutive stature belied her strength. My thoughts were confirmed when she began to tell me about her horse Honey and her life growing up on her family's farm, an upbringing that often builds a strong body and strong character.

Mollie was a natural storyteller. Her tales were rich in re-created scenes and conversations, all told in her distinctive twang and peppered with Southern expressions such as "daggum" and "ain't." "I was raised as an old-fashioned country girl," Mollie said. "We planted our own fields and tended our own crops when I was growing up. Seventy-three acres is a lot of land to maintain. I worked all the time, and I had to drop out of high school to keep the farm going because my dad got sick."

Most of the students I interviewed planned to pursue a companion animal track because they wanted to work with family pets, such as dogs and cats. But Mollie was interested in working with large animals, especially horses. She professed to love all animals, but she was unapologetic when she talked about little "ankle-biter" dogs. She preferred the "bully breeds"—large dogs like pit bulls and boxers who, she says, have a bad reputation. She and a friend used to run a bully breed rescue, which helped hone her skills in listening to animals and tempered her inclination to become attached to every animal who crossed her path.

In the farming world, losing animals is commonplace, and Mollie had learned from a young age that death was a part of life. Such stoicism is the norm among people who live and work on a farm. But unlike her family members and others in her farming community, Mollie was unwilling to shrug her shoulders and walk away from an animal in need, and she refused to think of animals solely in terms of their monetary value. She was devoted to preserving all life, including an animal's life, as much as she possibly could.

I admire Mollie's strength of character, pluck, and determination. The heart of Mollie's story—the part that moved me when I interviewed her and continues to move me—was her generous spirit and her desire to pay the love forward by helping people who are struggling to cope with an animal's illness or death.

Mollie

Honey was a quarter horse, papered and all. I showed her for five years, up until I was twenty-one. I had her for a long time, and she meant the world to me. She was a great horse.

Honey originally belonged to my godparents. One time I stopped by their place on my way to work, and I asked my godfather, "Hey, what's that one right there? When did you get her?" He told me he'd gotten her from a friend of a friend, and I said, "Oh, OK. I'm going to go see her then." And he was like, "Be careful. I already got kicked by her." But I went out there anyway, and right away she started nipping and pulling at my Carhartt. Most people would have made her stop, but my jacket was all torn up from living on a farm anyway, so I wasn't really worried about it. She was pulling on my jacket, and I just walked beside her and let her pull me around. She pulled me up to a bucket. I looked at the bucket, and she looked at me, and I looked back at her. Then she moved around broadside and looked at me again. I turned the bucket over, got up on it, put my arms up, and pressed down on her back. She didn't move. She just turned and looked at me like she was saying, "Get on and get up." I jumped up on her bare back, and the whole time I was hoping she wouldn't throw me. Then she just started walking around.

My godfather came out of the shop, shook his head, and said, "You got up on that horse!"

"Yep."

And he said, "How'd you do that? She won't let me on her. I don't know why. She let the daggum previous owner on her, but she won't let me on her."

I said, "That's because she don't like you."

And that's the way Honey was. She had her own ideas about things, including people.

I started going to see her all the time. Before I went to work, almost every day, I'd drive out and spend a couple of hours with her, ride her, clean her up, put her back in the barn, feed her, and then go to work. My godfather was a little worried about me spending a lot of gas money going out to his place all the time, and he wondered if my parents would approve. But I told him not to worry about it. It was my car and my money and all, so they didn't need to know. But then later when I was out of town, he talked with my parents and told them what I'd been doing. When I came back, Honey was at my house. She was my horse, my own personal horse. I didn't want to share her with anyone.

Honey wanted to play all the time. She was very, very playful, and she was full of life. I ain't never seen a horse with the personality she had, and I've been around horses all my life. If I wanted to get out of the house and relieve stress, nine times out of ten I was going out to the horse pasture. If I had homework or something, I'd go out there and lean up against a tree, and she would come up and look over my shoulder. She used to take my notebooks in her mouth and run off with them, and I'd have to chase her down. If I was cleaning out her stall and she was off in the pasture, she'd come into the stall and push me over. She was so funny. She was a real sweetheart.

I already had Honey when I got Buck, my pit boxer. He was a puppy when I got him, but even when he was little, I took him riding with Honey and me. He rode with me on the saddle until he got big enough to keep up, and then I started leashing him to the saddle. He would stay right with us. Even if I rode up to the store, he'd go along. I had to ride on a two-lane road with a ditch on each side, and I'd always put him over on the ditch side so I was closest to the road, and he wouldn't get hit or nothing. And Honey, she was so good. I would talk to her and leg-motion her while I was trying to keep up with him. If a car was coming, I'd say, "Honey, git dog," and she would turn around and nudge him back. She was like his mother, I would say, because she basically helped me raise that dog. They were my best friends. They really were.

Honey and I did a lot of horse shows and rodeos. We won a lot of shows. We won a saddle together. My favorite picture of us was at a rodeo. Depending on how high up you were in the standings, they'd give you a hat at the beginning of the rodeo. At the end of the rodeo, you can throw the hat out to the audience so they can have the hat you wore. Honey and I were riding around the arena, and I was holding the American flag. At the end of the round, I pulled her up. I squeezed my legs to let her know to "come up, baby," and she came up just as pretty as you could ask for. I went to throw the hat, and I wasn't holding the reins. I was just holding on to Honey with my legs, and my mama caught the perfect picture. Honey was rearing back, and my mama caught the picture just before I let go of my hat. It's the most beautiful picture I have of her.

Honey and I took trips too. We'd go up to the mountains, go camping for a whole weekend, and just ride. I'd pack up everything in the morning and ride all day, then unload and pitch everything back up. I went up with a couple of friends a few times, and then one time I went by myself because I was frustrated with life. Me and people don't get along very well most of the time. I can only take so much before I'm ready to pop someone's head or something. I was upset with life at the time, and I just went and picked up the trailer, put Honey up, and took off to the daggum mountains.

So yeah, Honey was my best friend. To me, animals aren't just animals. They're your friend. They're your better half sometimes. And that's what Honey was for me. That horse loved me to death, and I loved her.

• • •

When I was maybe eleven or twelve, I started helping my daddy and my uncle with birthing cows. One time, one of the baby cows came out clubfooted. And my uncle was like, "Well, that one ain't going to be worth nothing. Might as well go ahead and—"

But I'd just helped birth this cow, and I told my uncle, "You've lost your mind."

Now my daddy, he knew I wouldn't hear it, and he said to my uncle, "You know you're not going to be able to kill that calf around her."

The calf's clubfoot was bad but not that bad. I'd seen worse. I told my uncle I'd make a deal with him. I told him that every day, first thing in the morning, and every afternoon and every evening, I'd come up to his place and spend time with that calf, and I bet him that I'd have that calf walking normally in no time.

My uncle said, "You really want to do that? Well, that's OK. But if you don't come here three times a day, I'm going to take care of him, and that's all I'm going to say here."

So every morning at 4 a.m., I was down there. Every afternoon when I got off the school bus, I was down there. Every night before I went to bed, I was down there. I kept warm water on the calf's ankles and just constantly worked him. I made him put pressure on his club-foot, and I played with him so much that within about six months, he was walking. No problems.

My uncle gave me that cow. I named him Moose because I wanted him to grow big and strong. The funny thing was, Moose turned out to be one of the biggest cows we had. My uncle was like, "Can I have that cow back?" And I said, "No. He's mine. You can have him when he's old and ready to die."

When Moose started getting old and sick, I was like, yeah, I think it's about time for him to become supper. I told my daddy and uncle before they took him to the slaughterhouse that they had to mark the bags that had Moose in them. Because I wasn't going to eat that cow. When they took him up to the slaughterhouse, my dad told them, "Look, Mollie wants you to put Moose's name on the bags of meat." And the thing is, everyone knew the story of how Moose came about and all, and they were like, "This cow is Moose? Oh, man, I bet Mollie's not too happy about that." And my daddy said, "Not really. But she understands the way of life."

And that's the way it is on a farm. My dad calls it "the way of life." The way of life is that animals live, animals die. We don't like it. We're never going to like losing someone we care about.

But it's hard sometimes. I've always had a hard time when my animals died. When I was a little girl—maybe seven, eight years old—I had two ponies, and my favorite was named Charlie. Now, Charlie was old, and he wasn't doing too well, and one night when my mom got home from work, I told her that Charlie was sick and we had to save him. My dad was on his way home from work, which was about thirty-five, forty minutes away.

My mama called my dad and told him, "You gotta talk to Mollie. Charlie's not looking so good." And I screamed at my dad, "You gotta save him!"

But my dad never did call the vet because Charlie was old. It probably wouldn't have made any difference if the vet came out. The vet would probably have just gone ahead and euthanized him. But when you're eight years old and you're looking at your pony and he's dying, you still want to see an animal doctor there at least trying to save your pony. I understand my dad's point of view. I mean, we live on a farm. It's just like my daddy says. It's the way of life. Your animals die. But when you have an eight-year-old daughter whose heart's all wrapped up in that little pony, at least give her the satisfaction of trying to save the animal. One day I want to be able to do that.

• • •

After I left home, I always went back to the farm on Sundays to see Honey and take her and Buck out for a ride. Well, one Sunday I went over there, and I got the saddle and everything out, and then I went to the pasture to find Honey. I called and called and called. All the horses came up, but she never did. I was like, "Where in the world is Honey?"

My parents weren't home, so I called my mom, and the first thing she said was, "You at the house yet?"

I told her, "Yeah, I'm at the house. Where's Honey? I've been here for like thirty minutes trying to find her. Where is my horse?"

And my mama said, "We'll be home in five minutes."

I said, "No. You're going to tell me where my horse is. Did you sell my horse? What did you do with my horse? You tell me now. I'm not waiting until you get home."

Finally, she told me. She said, "Mollie, yesterday morning your dad was walking up to the mailbox, and Honey was lying down. He went over there to get her up because she didn't look like she was breathing, but she was already cold. Her body was already cold. She died on Friday night."

And that's when it hit me. We have a backhoe, and it was sitting there by the path to the barn. It's no big deal if it's out of the barn, but it was halfway in the ditch next to the path. It didn't really register with me when I first got to the house. I just thought my daddy might have been drunk or something when he was driving the backhoe, or my brother—he's an idiot, he can't drive it anyways. I didn't pay much attention to it. But when Mama told me what had happened, I knew that Daddy had already buried her. I knew I'd never see Honey again. My parents didn't call me on Saturday because I was working, and they didn't want me to skip a day at work. There wasn't anything I could have done, but it still made me mad that they didn't call to tell me. Because I didn't get to see her. I didn't get to say goodbye.

I'm not one who cries a lot. I don't show emotions very well. Everything turns into anger for me most of the time. When I got off the phone with my mama, I chucked my phone into the pasture, and I started yelling and screaming and hollering. Buck was running around in the pasture, still trying to find Honey. He was barking, but after a while, he went into a yippy bark. He was getting upset. I was sitting there on the ground, and he came over, sat right next to me, and put his paw on my shoulder. I said to him, "She's gone, baby." And that's when he got in my lap.

It was comforting in some sense. But then again, it hurt more because Buck looked so sad. It's like when a mother goes to a funeral with a kid, and it's not really about her emotions; it's more about the kid's emotions. You try to cover up your feelings so the kid knows it's OK. That's basically what I thought I was supposed to do with Buck. I tried to hide how I was feeling because, when I cry around him, he tends to start whimpering and getting upset. At first, I held it together and told him it was OK. Honey's gone, but it's OK. She's in a better place. But then he started whimpering and gave me that "I don't understand" look, and when I saw that, it really hurt, and I couldn't hold it back anymore. I just grabbed onto him and started bawling. It was like we both had to let it out.

But when my parents pulled in, that anger came back. I didn't say a word to them, though I'm sure the look on my face said plenty. I went to the hardware store, got a piece of wood, cut it out, stained it, sanded it, stained it again, and burned in "Rest in Peace, Honey. You'll always be in my heart."

• • •

I still ain't fully over losing Honey. It was a major hurt to me. She was my personal horse. She was my baby. Me and her went through so much together, and we knew each other so well. When she died, it tore me up. I never really understood when people said, "When a loved one died, I lost a part of me too." I never understood that until Honey died.

When Honey died, my family and friends couldn't really understand why I was so upset. My best friend rides horses and took riding lessons and all. But she didn't grow up with the passion for animals that I have. She likes them and she loves them, but there's no passion. And because I have such a passion for them, it hurts me so much more.

It's been two years since Honey died, and I still haven't gotten another quarter horse. I don't feel like I'm ready. My heart ain't ready for it. It's only in the past year or so that I've been able to see other horses and not relate them to Honey and start crying. I guess I've held onto the hurt for a long time. When she died, I thought if I forgot about her death, I was going to forget her, forget who she was. I didn't want to lose her memory. I mean, we've had horses die in the past. Yeah, it hurts to see them die. It hurts to bury them. But it was like, OK, it's the way of life. But after a couple of months, you forget about their death and how you felt, and you forget who they were as well. When you forget them when they died—forget who they were—in a year or two, you're not going to remember that horse. I think holding onto my hurt when Honey died was a way to hold onto the memories.

I still miss her. She still means the world to me. I like to go out to the farm and sit by her grave sometimes to do my homework or just get out of the house. It makes me happy to remember the good things, to remember the great horse she was. Lots of things remind me of her. I have a lot of pictures, and I have the saddle we won together. I also have her old horseshoes. I don't know why I decided to keep them because she had her shoes changed a lot, and we just threw them into a pile with the shoes from all the other horses. But for some reason, I decided to keep that set. They're a good set and could have been reused. But I'm not letting them go. I have one in the hallway, one in my bedroom, and two hanging on my bedpost. I've already mapped out where I'm going to put them when my fiancé and I move into the house we're redoing. I could hang them so they look like they're walking across the wall, going down the hallway.

Ever since I was a little kid, I wanted to work with animals. Animals tell you what they want. And that's why I feel like they're smarter than humans in some sense. I pay attention to what they want because so many people don't, and that's when you have unhappy animals. To me, animals are people. They're just fuzzy and on four legs. But they're still people. They're just a different type of person. Caring for animals is what I'm good at, and Honey and the other animals I've lost are a big part of why I want to be a vet tech. If you remember all the good times you've had with your animals, then it makes you work so much harder to save someone else's animal because you remember how it felt when one died on you.

Sometimes when I get stressed out over my classes and stuff, I'll look at Buck, at the other dogs I've had, and also at the pictures of Honey and me, and I'll be like, "Gotta do it." Because there's going to be a little girl one day. I can just see it. There's going to be a little girl who loves her little pony so much, and her pony's going to be sick. Her mom and dad are going to call the veterinarian and me, and I'll want to save that pony for that little girl. So, basically, I want to do for someone else what couldn't be done for me.

CHAPTER 6

Rachel and Raffi

It was almost like it was just the two of us in
our own world, and everybody else didn't really
exist at that time. Raffi was always next to me. He
taught me a sense of friendship.

— Rachel

Rachel arrived for our interview wearing pressed jeans and a crisp, long-sleeved oxford shirt. Friendly and animated, she proved to be an enthusiastic and loquacious storyteller. Of the roughly nineteen thousand words in the interview transcript, only about six hundred were mine. With so much to say, Rachel seemed driven to share her story about her childhood dog, a yellow lab named Raffi.

Many of the students I spoke with discussed pets they'd had as children. These relationships shaped their identities as animal lovers, instilling lifelong lessons in reciprocity, kindness, and responsibility for another living being. Rachel credited Raffi with teaching her what it means to be a good friend. And although it had been many years since she lost Raffi, she'd maintained a connection with him.

Rachel's story demonstrates that it is often through our friendships with pets that we discover who we are. For Rachel, her friendship with Raffi nurtured her natural affinity for animals, which blossomed into a deeply felt concern for animal welfare and a decision to enter the veterinary profession. In doing so, Rachel discovered kindred spirits among her fellow animal caregivers, which she'd struggled to find in her family of origin.

Rachel

Raffi was the very first pet I had the pleasure of owning. I'm the big animal lover in my family, so I was the one who begged for a dog. My parents let me and my sister pick him out, and I picked Raffi. I was only about three, but I remember it clearly. There were all these puppies, and they all looked the same, but they acted differently. Some were eating, some were sleeping, some were off by themselves, and some were running around. Raffi was the rowdy one. He wanted to play with everyone, and I was like, "OK, I want him!"

Labs are very good dogs—very playful and very silly but very protective too. I think that was the first time I realized I enjoyed having the company of a dog, because there were times when my parents were always working, and they didn't have time to entertain me and my sister. I learned to take Raffi out, play with him, teach him little things. When my parents weren't home, my sister and I used to run back and forth in the house and let him chase us. Anywhere we went or whatever we did, he would do that too. If I ran around in a circle and jumped on the couch, he would do the same thing. It was like he was mimicking what we were doing. We would hide behind the couch sometimes and pull it back to where he couldn't get to us. He knew we were back there, and it would just drive him crazy. And then when he finally did get to us, he was like, "Oh my gosh! I found you!" And he'd jump up and down. Of course, my parents didn't know that we did stuff like that because we would have gotten in trouble. But I thought it was so much fun.

I'd talk to Raffi just like I would talk to a friend. I knew he wasn't going to talk back, but I really did feel that he loved me. Raffi taught me to use my imagination. He allowed me to be a child. I had somebody to pretend with, somebody to play with, someone who took my attention off whatever was going on in my household. It was like, "OK, they're arguing. Let's close the door, and we'll just play together." It was just the two of us in our own world, and everybody else didn't really exist at that time. He taught me a sense of friendship. He was my baby doll, and like most girls, I liked to play with Barbies and dress them up, so that's what I did with Raffi. When you're playing and having fun as a child and you have a pet who will let you put hats on him and do silly things and not try to move away from you—it's so much fun. I didn't have someone judging me or telling me, "You're acting crazy," or "Hats don't belong on dogs." For me, those things were just pure, innocent fun. Maybe at the time, Raffi didn't like it. I could have been getting on his last nerve, but he never responded that way. He was super patient with me.

Whatever I wanted to do was OK with Raffi. Obviously, I was in control of the show at the time. I was the one making all the decisions and having fun, and he was going along with it. He let me be all over him, all the time, doing whatever I wanted to, and he never left my side. If I got up and walked somewhere, he followed me. If I came back, he followed me. He was attached to me just like I was attached to him. It wasn't one of those things like, "I'll get to you when I get to you, after I've done this and this and this, and then I'll play with you." That's how it is for parents who are always busy with things. But Raffi was always next to me.

• • •

My family moved a lot when I was a kid. After we got Raffi, we moved a few times, and then we moved out West, where most of our family is from. We stayed with one of our family members, and he let us bring Raffi. He had his own house, so Raffi had a backyard, and they had a black lab called Thor. Raffi and Thor used to play together, and my cousins and I would run wild in their backyard. But then my dad got a job in another state, and we had to move again. We had to leave Raffi behind, and that was very hard for me because I had been with him for so long. I'd had Raffi for about five years at that point.

We left Raffi with a friend of my father's when we moved. My dad tried to comfort me, and my dad's friend also talked to me because he knew I was attached to Raffi. My dad's friend assured me that he would take care of Raffi and that he knew and understood how much I cared about him. My dad and his friend told me, "You know, you're going to have another pet someday." They also told me, "It's going to get better. It's not always going to be this painful." And it was comforting, at least at the time, to know that my dad and his friend cared about me and how I was feeling. They loved me, so I knew they loved Raffi too. And my dad's friend telling me that he would take care of Raffi meant a lot to me because I trusted him. But something happened—I don't know what—and my dad's friend couldn't keep Raffi anymore, and he gave him away.

Once I found out that Raffi wasn't with my dad's friend anymore, I was worried. I remember wondering where he was. I never knew what happened to him after that. I knew he had a home, but my parents tried to wean me from asking questions about him so I wouldn't get my feelings hurt if maybe he died. My parents never let me find out where he was or try to go see him because they felt like he wasn't our pet anymore. He belonged to someone else, so they felt it was best to not meddle or try to go back.

After we moved away, we'd go back periodically to visit because that's where my grandparents lived. My aunt who lived out there told me several times that my dad's friend had given Raffi to someone to use as a guard dog, like at an auto garage where the dog stays outside. I think she was teasing me because when she told me he was a guard dog, she was like, "He's very mean now, and I don't think you should see him," which stunk because why would you tease somebody about something like that, especially a little kid?

I always felt like Raffi would have remembered me. He probably was angry because we left him and didn't come back. Once an animal makes a bond with you and then they're taken away from you, I think they do wait for you to come back for them. That was hurtful. I worried that he was still waiting for me. That's a lot for a dog to go through, just like any person. Imagine what it would be like if you were taken from your house and then your owners left and the person you were playing with all the time who really showed you love was gone and you got stuck in a place where you're an outside dog and there are no children around. I'm sure it was just adults who were hollering at him and telling him what to do. I've seen people who treat animals like they're just animals. I don't think if you turn a family dog into a guard dog there's a lot of loving going on there. That was one thing that hurt my feelings—knowing he wasn't being treated as a family member, like he literally was being stuck out in the cold. And I didn't know if whoever had him was being nice to him in the way I was nice to him. I couldn't save him from that. I couldn't break him out and say, "OK, Raffi. We're going to run away together."

Losing Raffi like that was hard for me. It hurt leaving him and never knowing what happened to him. I still feel grief over the fact that I never got a chance to see him or even know if he was being treated the right way. If you get attached to a pet or a person, you don't ever want to have that loved one just completely disappear because then you make up all these things in your mind, like, "I wonder if he's roaming the highways." I used to have these nights after we left Raffi when I would think to myself, "Well, what if I could just have Daddy take me down there, and we could get him back and put him in the car, and he could just stay in my room." Or I would imagine that I would just be walking down the street one day, and he would be there, and I would recognize him. Then I would barter with whoever was with him and do whatever it took to get him back.

I was very animated as a child, and I'm still very silly at times, or I just have a very vivid imagination. So yeah, I plotted to rescue my dog. [laughs] But then, of course, when I thought about it, I was like, "My parents would kill me." They would have had a fit. Because I'm silly like that. I do things sometimes where my parents are like, "It's just a dog. What is wrong with you?"

I think at first we got Raffi for my dad, but because I spent so much time with him, he became my dog. I mean, I was the one who took care of him. I was the one who was attached to him. I think my dad likes the idea of having a dog more than actually having one and taking care of it. My father is one of those people who will get a dog because he wants a dog to guard the house, or because he wants to train him and have the dog do what he tells him to do. I guess it's a manly thing. Now, my mom, she's not a dog person whatsoever. My mom cannot stand dog hair, and she doesn't like licking; she doesn't like any of that. I get such a kick out of it. Here she is trying to doll me up, make me look like a girl, and tell me not to touch the dog. "Don't touch him!" she'd say. "Now you're going to have to wash your hands." My older sister was the same way. She didn't like to be licked, and she hates dog hair. In my family, I always felt like I was supposed to keep Raffi close to me.

What it comes down to is that my parents were never pet people. They were always working, so I don't think they really looked at pets as family members. It took me constantly telling them that this dog is my baby for them to get it and really understand that you can have a relationship or a bond with an animal. It was hurtful because I thought about animals differently than they did.

As a child, you can't control things like that. Your parents are in full control of everything that goes on. I didn't ask for a dog for a long time after we left Raffi. I thought that my parents put money and their jobs over their child and that my relationship with Raffi didn't matter enough to them. Now that I'm older, though, I've come to terms with it. It was not a good feeling to have to give him up, and it took me a long time to get to the point where I could accept my parents' decision to leave him behind.

• • •

I understand my parents, but I'm not like them. If I choose to buy my daughter a pet, then that pet will be a permanent part of the family. I don't want to get a dog just to see my kid smile, without thinking about the reality of taking care of it or whether I can afford it. And that's usually what happened every time my parents got a pet. Every time we moved, my family would say, "OK, we can get a dog now, because we're settled in and we need one." But ultimately, nobody in my family wanted to take care of our pets. I pitched in and did those things. I didn't mind because I really do enjoy taking care of my dogs. If somebody scolded the dog or yelled at him, I would say, "Don't talk to him like that. Don't yell at him." I'm still like that.

I've had friends who would get dogs just to get them, and I would say, "Why do you keep getting animals when you don't like animals? You don't really like having dogs." I tell my friend this all the time. It's probably not funny, but I tell her all the time, "If I were not your friend, I would definitely call the ASPCA on you." Because for some people, getting animals is almost like collecting. It's not really about the animal at all. It's almost as if the animal is an accessory, like a colored watch band or a handbag. For some people, it's not necessarily an attachment to the animal they have. It's more like, "I have a dog that looks vicious," or "I have a dog that looks like a little stuffed animal." Some people do look at animals that way. I've grown up with family members who are like that. They'll continue to get dogs, and if one dies from parvo or from being malnourished or something, they think, "Oh, it's just a dog. Dogs get sick, and it's not something you can control. There's nothing you can do about it. It's God's will." And maybe that's true. But if you don't feed a living thing or water a living thing, and if you don't bathe it or take care of that animal, then it's your fault. Animals are like children. You chose to have them. They did not choose you.

My attitude is, if you can't take care of your dog, then you don't need one. People need to understand that having a pet is a big responsibility. Don't bite off more than you can chew. Have some humility. If you can't afford seven or eight dogs, you don't need seven or eight dogs, especially if you don't have the space for that many pets. And if you can't afford to take care of them and get them regular checkups, it's best not to get them. These animals are living beings. They're not a stuffed toy that you can just pick up and play with when you want to. You have to take care of that animal. You have to put in the time and effort to train animals so they're well socialized. You also have to think about where you are in your life because you can't show an animal love when you're stressed out and angry at the world because you can't get the things you want.

Sometimes I feel like I have to show other people that animals are not just these objects that have no idea what love is or what it means to have comfort or joy. Having a pet is just like having a child. We all know they don't live forever, and they don't necessarily grow up to do big things like your child might. But they do play a huge role in your household because of the mood and energy they bring. I've learned from my animals. I think that as long as you do right by animals, they will do right by you. Maybe it's just a universal code, like when you do right, and you do good by others, and just living things in general, then that same energy comes back to you.

· · ·

Having such a good relationship with Raffi made me appreciate the bond you can have with an animal, which pushed me to want to learn more about them, and that pushed me to want to help them. When I got to that point, I almost felt stuck. I hate watching TV, but I could watch animal shows all day long, and sometimes it was so hard to see how cruel people could be to animals. For a while, knowing there were people like that kept me from pursuing this career. When I watched shows like *Animal Cops*, I would get so frustrated and mad, and I'd think, "Why do people do this?"

But then I started to see that there were so many different avenues you could go down to help animals, and it changed the way I looked at it. I started to be able to separate myself from people who are cruel to animals and focus instead on those who love animals. Being in vet tech school and doing my observation hours at a clinic—it was nice to see some of us share a camaraderie. We like taking care of pets, understanding that they're family members. We care about their health and life span and what we can do to make sure they have healthy lives. It's nice to know that I'm going to fit somewhere in that world and be able to help. When I'm in the clinic, I know that all the people in the room have the same love for what they're doing and for their personal pets, just like I had that same love for Raffi. You know, we all get it. We all understand what we're here for.

With my work, I can bond with other people's animals. It's as if I'm working at a day care and taking care of someone else's children. They're like babies. This profession is really showing me how important it is to treat your animals—all animals—with kindness.

I think my bond with Raffi is never going away. It's been fifteen years since I lost him, but I still remember him. He's had a big impact on my life and will always be embedded in my mind. It's not something I have to conjure up. It's a good feeling. Raffi was like my first love. I like to keep the memory of Raffi the way he was so that I don't have to think about whether he might have become a guard dog or all those other things I imagined might have happened to him. I just try to remember the good things—that he was mine when he was mine, and I loved him. Raffi helped me become who I am. I'm an animal lover. I'm a dog lover. I love Raffi even though I don't have him anymore. Those things are a part of who I am. He brought out that love for taking care of animals and bonding with them. He's the reason I love animals so much.

CHAPTER 7

Celeste and Rambo

I wanted to go into animal rescue because of what
I saw Rambo and other animals go through. It's like
seeing an abused child. I can't handle that.

— Celeste

I met Celeste at a pancake house near the college early on a Monday morning. For more than an hour and a half, she shared her story over multiple cups of coffee. A divorced mother of three grown children, Celeste was middle-aged and unassuming in appearance. Her gray-peppered hair was drawn back in a ponytail, she was dressed comfortably in a T-shirt and jeans, and she wore no makeup. She seemed nervous at the beginning of our interview, but once she started talking about animals, her demeanor changed. Her eyes brightened, and she became very animated.

Celeste said she was an "animal person," a term that carries different meanings in our society. For some people, being an animal person is simply a matter of loving animals or perhaps having a pet you're particularly attached to. But for Celeste, being an animal person has more to do with her special affinity for animals and her ability to communicate with them. "I think an animal person is born with instincts on how to relate with animals," she said. "Knowing how to talk to them and build a bonded relationship is inborn. It's just like somebody who's born with a talent for math or art. You're just born with it."

Celeste's story about her dog Rambo is painful to read, but it's also brutally honest, and I'm grateful to Celeste for being so open about Rambo's tragic death. Her narrative shows that, among the many emotions and sensations we might experience when we lose a beloved, guilt is one of the most common and intractable. The reasons for this phenomenon are complex, but one of the most obvious is that our animals are childlike. They're innocents, and as their guardians, we're responsible for speaking for them and making life-and-death decisions on their behalf. If they suffer at the end of their lives or their lives are cut short, we often blame ourselves, even when there was little we could do to change their fate.

Through her work in animal rescue and as a vet tech, Celeste seemed to be seeking atonement for Rambo's suffering, but she was also empowering herself where she felt powerless. Her work helping animals defines her identity and, indeed, her very reason for being on this earth. "I think I was put on the earth like St. Francis or Noah or somebody like that, where I think my whole job on Earth is to help the animals," she said. "And that's it. That's all I'm here for."

Celeste

Ever since I was little, from as early as I remember, I've talked to animals. If I went to the zoo, I would talk with the animals. My dad thought I was crazy. For me, my stuffed animals were alive. I was like Dr. Dolittle. I would doctor them, feed them, water them with real water. My stuffed animals became my friends, and then when I got real animals, they became my friends, and I felt like I could talk to them, like I could get on their level so they understood me. That has never gone away.

I've always felt a connection with animals. I'm not going to lie. It's the only thing I've got. I can't tell anybody that because they'll think I'm crazy. But I feel like there's a connection there. Sometimes it's an unspoken connection. The animal just knows. An animal can figure out if you're nervous or not. They look at you to see what's inside you, and if that animal sees something good inside you, you get that vibe back. But if you're mean and have a negative attitude, they pick it up very quickly and won't trust you. You have to earn their trust before you can build a relationship with a pet. I think that just comes naturally to me.

When I look into a dog's eyes, I feel like I'm looking into their soul. I can see something beyond the fur on the outside. There's more to an animal than their fur or feathers. They have a soul. Most people don't believe that, but I believe there's more to an animal than just the outside. They have a brain and a heart, and they deserve to be respected and protected.

I think my desire to help animals started when I was about four years old. My parents and I were driving out to the country to visit family. It was a rainy day, and a little yellow bird hit the windshield. I started screaming because the bird was hurt, and my dad pulled over, ran out into traffic, picked up the little bird, and brought it back into the car. I begged him to let me hold it, so he put the bird in something and let me hold him. When we got to our family's place out in the country, my dad and I put the bird down by a tree, and when we came back, he had died. Dad explained that God decided to take him to heaven. Of course, I was upset. I was just little. I was mad because I couldn't do anything to help the bird. Even as a four-year-old, I knew I was going to do something with my life to help animals.

Animals are special because they give you unconditional love. Any animal that you really take care of will love you unconditionally—a lot more than a person can sometimes. I'm not saying all the time, because you can get close to people too. I've never had a person give me unconditional love, but my animals have. An animal can get you through things you've never dreamed of. They can calm you down. They can express how they feel about you, they seem to understand what you're going through, and they're always there to help you out. My dachshund will crawl up on me when I'm sitting on the couch and just go to sleep right on top of me. The lab I have now acts like he hasn't seen me for ten years every time I walk through the door. He about knocks me over every time. He runs up to me and jumps all over me just because I came home.

· · ·

For a long time, my husband—now ex-husband—wouldn't let me have animals. He believed animals belonged outside, and I didn't. My ex also didn't believe in taking animals to a vet. He wouldn't spend any money on animals.

One time we took in a dog that belonged to my husband's aunt because they were too old to take care of him. My husband made us chain him up outside. I hated it, but there was nothing I could do about it. The dog was a husky, and my son got attached to him. Well, one day we found him bleeding out of his mouth. He probably had heartworms or something. He would bite and be ferocious because he was in so much pain. He was digging a hole, and he was trying to hide in it, and I couldn't get near him, or he would try to bite. I didn't know what he had for sure, so I had to make the kids stay away from him. Eventually, he died, and my kids and I buried him. That husky was my son's first dog.

I also had rabbits. My ex would make them stay outside in the heat, in the hundred-degree heat, in a little cage, and they died. I'm from up north, and I very quickly learned that you can't keep animals outside down south. Looking back, there's no way I'd do that again.

I never gave up on my dream of having a dog of my own, and I kept trying to find a way to convince my ex to let me get one. As it turned out, I took care of my father-in-law for three years before he died. It was a rough time caring for him with three toddlers and whatnot. After that, my husband finally allowed me to get a dog, though I had to pay for him myself. He was extra special because not only did I go through taking care of my ex's dying father, but I also had to come up with my own money to pay for the puppy. I always wanted to get a little schnauzer so that's what I did. When I first got him, he was this furry little ball that just fit in my hand. He looked so innocent that I named him Rambo so he would be tough. And he was.

Over the years, my marriage didn't go so well, and my ex started hitting me. When the physical abuse started, Rambo would bite my ex for trying to hit me, and that got him mad at the dog. Rambo also peed on his free weights sometimes, and my ex would be furious, and he'd punch Rambo. I'd defend Rambo and then get hit because I was defending the dog. I also told my husband that I liked Rambo better than him. It was a bad situation for all of us. Rambo ended up bloody sometimes, and I couldn't handle that.

When I finally decided to leave, I had Rambo and a little dachshund puppy. But I couldn't take both because I couldn't afford the fees at the apartment I'd rented. It was the hardest choice I ever had to make. Who do I take? Do I take the dachshund puppy, or do I take my Rambo, who I loved to death? I ended up taking the puppy and leaving Rambo because he was older, and I thought he would be able to fend for himself a little better than the puppy. I prayed that my ex wouldn't hurt Rambo after I was gone. I found out later that as soon as I left, my ex immediately threw Rambo outside and chained him up. Rambo wasn't used to being outside, so I know it had to be rough on him.

When I'd saved enough money, I came back to get Rambo, but my ex wouldn't let me have him. He said Rambo was a family dog, and he was going to stay there no matter what. I thought about taking my ex to court about it, but I didn't have the money. And two of my kids still lived with my ex, and Rambo was still their dog, and I couldn't just steal him. I couldn't rightly do that.

But then my ex went on vacation, and at some point the neighbors found Rambo dead on the side of the road. When they told my ex that Rambo had died when he was gone, he didn't care, and they ended up burying Rambo. That's about it. I didn't hear exactly what happened. The kids didn't hear much.

When I found out Rambo had died, I felt a ton of grief run over me. I was horrified. I tried to apologize to him. I felt like I failed him because I couldn't take him with me. I felt like I let him down. All I could do was pray that he's up in heaven and has the freedom to run around and do all the things I wished he could have done down here. I hope that Rambo doesn't hold it against me because I couldn't take him with me.

Nobody really understood how I felt after Rambo died. No one else had that connection to him, except maybe my son, but he was so little I had to be strong for him. No one would talk to me. I wasn't close to my mother, and she wasn't an animal person. My sisters would just say, "Well, you'll get over it. Get another pet." Or friends would say, "Yeah, I'm sorry you're going through this, but you'll get over it." And that's about all I heard. There was no consolation. There was no real burial or anything. Eventually, I just gave up. There was nobody I could reach out to for something like that. I think the closest was my dad because he was an animal lover, but he was already gone when Rambo died. I like to think that any animal of mine who has passed is in my dad's arms right now. My sister's dog died a couple of weeks ago, and I pictured her dog running to my dad and jumping into his arms.

Come to think of it, though, I wasn't completely alone when I lost Rambo. I had my dachshund puppy, and I'm sure I talked to him. I still talk to my pets about Rambo. I tell them about the good things Rambo did and what a great dog he was. I tell them how much they would have loved him if he were still around—just like someone who talks to you about a person in their life. The world wouldn't be the same without animals. I talk to my animals about animals. I talk to them about how good they are, what they did for me, and what good things we can do together.

. . .

It still hurts to think about Rambo and how he died. It will always hurt. I don't think it will ever go away. But I try to remember the good things that happened. I remember looking into his eyes as a puppy and how fun and joyful he was and how licky he was. And then I looked into his eyes again when he was older, and I saw the cataracts, and I realized that he and I had a special bond because we'd known each other for so long and been through so much together. He's in my heart all the time. I think about the happy things, and I think about how much better off he is in heaven. I believe the animals who have passed know when you're thinking about them. I think the bond is as strong as you have with animals on Earth. I think you keep that connection going the rest of your life.

Someday, I'll see all my animals that have passed. I'll have my dachshund, my guinea hens, my rabbits, cats, dogs, ferrets, fish, and any other animals I've had. About any animal you can think of, I've had. I'll have quite a zoo when I get up there. I think when you get to heaven, you can communicate with your animals like you wish you could here. To hear Rambo say, "I understand, and I love you" would be the best thing that could ever happen.

Sometimes it's a relief not to know how Rambo died. Maybe it would be worse knowing how he died and what he suffered. But I know if I stuck my marriage out, I would have ended up in the hospital. I was trying to protect my kids and my dogs, and I protected them equally. My ex never hit the kids but once. Then that never happened again. But the dogs he continued to abuse, and I swore I would get away from him, and I would rescue every dog, every animal I could, in the name of my pets that didn't make it. I went into animal rescue because of what I saw Rambo and other animals go through. It's like seeing an abused child. I can't handle that. For some reason, animals hit me harder than people do because there's help for people. There's not so much help for abused animals, and I want to be the one to go in there and rescue those animals, like on those TV shows where people rescue animals from terrible situations. I would pick the animals up and hug them and let them know they're safe.

When an animal is sick or dying, there may not be anything you can do for them at that point, but you're still trying to give them some respect and admiration. You're trying to let the animal know you care that they're alive. A lot of people don't do that for animals these days. A dog will cross the road or a turtle or something, and I always try to get the animal out of the road. A lot of people, when there's a squirrel or whatever, would just as soon run them over rather than slow down.

There's a lot of trust that an animal has to give a vet tech because you handle them a lot, and you do things to them they don't like. If you respect them and go slow and let them know you care, they'll calm down and let you help them out. If not, they'll fight. That's just the animal instinct. Their fight-or-flight response is faster than ours, and they'll fight whatever you're trying to do because they're scared. You have to let them know you're not trying to hurt them. I decided to go into veterinary technology so I can help animals and understand them even more than I have in the past. The more knowledge I have, the more I can help them.

⟡

CHAPTER 8

Jane, Rudy, Sam-Sam, and Ariel

When I was a little girl, my mom and I were
out walking, and we came across this tiny bird. I
remember feeling like there wasn't much I could do
to help the bird. . . .
I wanted to know more. If I knew more, maybe I
could help more.

— Jane

All the vet tech students I interviewed said they'd always loved animals, and many said they knew from a very young age they wanted to work with them. This was Jane's experience as well. A calm, studious young woman, she told me she had been fascinated by animals from her earliest memories and was very motivated to learn about them and the proper ways to care for them. She was studying veterinary technology as a first step toward a veterinary degree, and she hoped someday to specialize in animal behavior to better understand the connection between behavior and health.

Although Jane described several pets who were special to her—including a dog named Rudy, a cat named Sam-Sam, and a rat named Ariel—it was clear that her passion for her work was driven less by her bond with a particular pet than by her strong desire to master the science of veterinary medicine. For Jane, knowledge was power; the more she learned, the more she could help animals in need. Some of her fellow students mentioned this as well, but my conversation with Jane tended to veer strongly toward science and her desire to keep learning and share her technical knowledge with her peers. She exhibited deep compassion and intellectual curiosity in equal measure.

Jane

My interest in animals began with this random bird. I was a little girl, maybe seven or eight years old. My mom and I were out walking, and we came across this tiny bird that must have fallen out of its nest. It might have been a sparrow.

I remember feeling like I couldn't really help the bird. We couldn't tell if the bird was hurt because we didn't know anything about it. We just put it in a little container with some bedding and tried to keep it warm. My mom was calling everywhere trying to figure out what to do with it. The bird had its mouth open, as if it were hungry. I remember feeling like there wasn't much I could do to help the bird, and I was worried about it. We took it to a wildlife refuge, but it didn't make it.

About two years later, we got our dog Rudy. I was ten years old. We got him from a shelter when he was maybe six months old. It was actually his euthanasia date. When we first got him, Rudy was very shy, like maybe he'd been abused or something. We had to hand-feed him until he got used to the food, but he learned pretty quickly. He was very food-motivated and a people-type dog. He wanted to be around us all the time. We walked him in the backyard, and whenever we met people, he would want to play with them. My mom was always worried about that. She really wanted him to be a guard dog because we didn't have a fence out back. But he wasn't a guard dog because, overall, he was very friendly. He loved people, and we've always had a cat, and he loved cats too. I think he liked other dogs, though it was hard to say because he wasn't around other dogs a lot. We got another dog later on, and he liked that dog.

When we first got Rudy, I remember wanting to learn as much as possible about dogs. I read every book in the library about dogs. I learned about dog breeds, about his personality, his temperament, and how he learns. I wanted to be sure I was taking care of him well, like walking him and training him. Well, I tried to train him, though I was just figuring it out, and I was pretty young. I taught him the basics like sit, come, and lie down.

Rudy was the first animal I really learned a lot about, but my first pet was a cat with a weird name, Sam-Sam. Well, he was my mom's pet. She saved him from some kids who were throwing rocks at him. He was just a kitten. She got him a couple of months before I was born, so he was there my entire life, for all my childhood. My mom told me she was nervous about having me because I was her first child. So she said, "OK, if I can be with this cat and do well, it will be fine." She always says Sam-Sam was her first baby.

I learned how to interact with animals through Sam-Sam, like what was OK and what wasn't. He didn't act like a typical cat. He acted more like a dog than a cat. His favorite food was potatoes. My mom worked at McDonald's when she got him, and he loved taking her fries. Anytime there were chips, french fries, or mashed potatoes around, Sam-Sam always wanted some. He was always around us. Whenever you were in the bathroom, he wanted to be in there with you. It didn't matter if the door was closed or not. But, weirdly enough, he didn't like to be held. My sister and I didn't care. We would try to hold him anyway. We have a lot of pictures of us trying to hold him, but it's clearly not going well. You just had to let him do his own thing.

He was a good cat. He would sleep on my bed in my room. If I was afraid, I'd want him in there. Usually, he'd come with me when I went to bed at night and stay with me until I fell asleep. I remember one time, I was almost asleep, and he peeked at my face to see if I was awake. I opened my eyes when he left the room, so I knew he was watching out for me.

It hurt a lot when Sam-Sam passed. I was a senior in high school. Like I said, he had been there for my entire life, so it was like losing a family member. I knew life would be very different without him, and I didn't want to lose him.

We knew he was sick because he had thyroid issues, but I thought he was getting better. The vet did a house call the day before Sam-Sam passed. He was very dehydrated, so they gave him a lot of fluids and an injection of pain meds. The next day, my sister and I were at school, and my dad was home with my stepsister, who was visiting for Thanksgiving. They went to the store and came back, and Sam-Sam was breathing heavily. My dad called my mom and told her, but by the time she got there, he was already gone. Then when I got home from school, they told me what happened. It was hard because I thought he was getting better.

The night before Sam-Sam passed, I remember talking to a friend on the phone about him. I was crying, and he came over and sat with me. So that was good. I also talked to a family member who said something like, "Oh, he had a good life"—that kind of thing. I mean, that's true. He was loved. He was a rescue, so he had a better life than he would have if he hadn't been rescued.

I also rescued a rat named Ariel. She was a white rat, an albino. I rescued her because her owner was trying to get rid of her. Nobody wanted her, so he was going to donate her to science at the school. And I was like, "I don't want you to do that." So I took her.

When I first got her, I did research about rats. I didn't realize they were so smart. She was really smart. She knew her name, and she'd come to me when I called her. I would let her out in the house, but only when my roommates weren't there because they didn't like her. A lot of people are afraid of rats. People think their tails are gross, but I didn't feel like that. I'd be open to another one someday. She was a great pet overall. I had no idea rats could be such great pets. Now, when the right occasion comes up, I talk about Ariel. I was with a friend in a pet store the other day, and I mentioned Ariel because there were rats in the store. She was like, "Oh, rats are nasty." I tried to correct her misperception. She still doesn't believe me, but I tried. [laughs]

I got Ariel during a major transition in my life, when I was going from high school to college. I felt like, at one point, she was my only friend, and when she passed, it was pretty hard. She died of a tumor, and at the time I didn't know tumors were so common in rats. I was hand-feeding her with droppers, but she had stopped taking the food, and I was afraid I'd come home one day, and she would have died alone. I decided to have her euthanized. I took Ariel's death hard. I couldn't bring myself to clean out her cage. It was in my car for a while, maybe like a week or two, because I just didn't want to look at it.

I talked to my mom when Ariel died, but I didn't talk to anyone else. My roommates asked where she was because they lived with her, but I didn't say much about it. The day she was euthanized, I was supposed to go to work, but I just didn't want to be at work. My manager sent me home because I was really sad, really upset. I worked at a small Hallmark store, and the next day, my manager got me a little card and a flower. That was nice. I didn't talk to most people, though, because I just didn't think they would understand, I guess mostly because she was a rat. If she had been a dog, maybe some people would understand that you'd be sad. But Ariel wasn't a typical pet.

• • •

My mom and I have had a lot of pets. We still have a lot of pets. Right now, I have one cat who is my personal cat. I just want to throw that out there. Well, actually, I own one and a half cats. One is my old roommate's cat, but she couldn't take her when we moved out, so my mom was like, "What's one more cat?" Which is part of the problem. We currently have nine cats and two dogs. Three of the cats were babies we hand-raised, and two of them we got as kittens off Craigslist after another cat passed away.

I also worked at a kill shelter, one of those shelters where they kill for space. It was one of my first animal care jobs. For some reason, nobody wanted to adopt black cats. There was one black kitten, and her whole litter got adopted, but she and her brother were left. Her brother got sick and died, and she was the only one left. Everybody at the shelter loved her. She would meet me in the hallway every morning when I came to work. I felt like she picked me, so when I left that job, I took her with me. Legally, she's mine, but my mom was like, "Well, she's part of the family now." I can't really get her back.

And then last November, my mom was coming home from work, and the neighbor across the street told her, "I think your cat's been out all day." We had five cats at the time, and my mom was like, "Oh, my gosh! Which cat?" Eventually, we saw her, but she wasn't one of our cats. Still, this cat had been sitting at our door all day, waiting to come in, like she knew it was a good place to be. My mom was like, "OK, she can come in because it's cold." She came in, and my mom said, "We'll keep her until we get her spayed." We got her spayed, and then my mom was trying to find a home for her, but that didn't work out, so now she's here to stay.

All the animals are taken care of. They all have their shots and are spayed and neutered, so there are no babies. But I tell my mom that we're at max capacity. Taking care of all those animals is a lot of work. Feeding everybody and walking the dogs takes at least an hour. My mom started this rescue thing, and I'm grateful for that. I've learned a lot of compassion from my mom. She's a nurse, so I've learned a lot from her. She's also helped me a lot by sharing her medical knowledge and showing me what I can do to help the animals when they're sick. People and animals are similar from a medical perspective. My mom has been a big influence on me, and I didn't really realize that until talking with you.

Rescuing animals and helping them—it's just great. Right now, we have three of the babies my mom and I raised, and they're five years old. It's cool to know where they began. One of them was lost in a trash plant, and I'm sure the mom was around, but they only found the kitten, and he was less than a day old, maybe a few hours. They didn't think he would make it, but he did. And that just feels really good.

• • •

I used to be a foster mom for kittens through a shelter where I worked. I'll never forget those kittens. I got them when they were maybe a month old. I was basically their mom. I bottle-fed them every two hours and kept them clean and warm. But they were sickly. We think they had panleukopenia, which is a virus that's really contagious and can be fatal. It was hard watching them get sick, putting all that effort into keeping them alive, then watching them decline food, knowing what's about to happen, and there's nothing you can do to stop it. I found two of them dead. I think the one who survived knew what had happened. He jumped on me and was meowing, like he knew something was wrong. It's interesting.

That experience was pretty hard, but I learned a lot. I learned that panleukopenia is a kitten disease. Most cats don't get it. The first time I encountered that disease, I was getting advice from my coworkers at the rescue, but I was still learning what to expect, especially before it got bad. I learned what I can do more of. Caring for those kittens and losing two of them was an empowering experience, even though it was hard. It gave me more confidence, and I know I'll be able to help more since I've seen the disease before.

My interest in veterinary medicine is really about all the animals I've known, even the ones I didn't mention. When I find out an animal has an illness, I want to know what I can do to help. I like finding new things to do. I have a lot of books about feline disease now—books about all kinds of situations. I talk to my coworkers and the other vet tech students too. I like helping people. I talk to them about the animals I've had and share information with them about what worked and what didn't.

I've also talked with my coworkers about how to cope with different situations. Some of them talked about how they dealt with losses like the kittens dying of panleukopenia. One person's story really helped me because I felt like we handled the loss of the cats in the same way, and we felt the same way about it. She was saying how much time and effort she put into trying to save them, and hers didn't make it either. She talked about how she cried. Knowing that other people felt the same way as me helped me.

I think the biggest thing for me—the thing that helps me the most—is the learning. I got into this field first as a kennel technician to help the animals. But I didn't have enough information, like it was only basic care, and I was thrown into that job, even though I wasn't really working on the medical side. I had to learn by trial and error. Because I was already interested in animals and medicine, it made me want to see what I could do, medically speaking. I'm always looking for more. I just want to be sure I'm doing everything I can. With Sam-Sam, I remember watching him walk around with this big saline hump they get when you give them fluids, thinking, "I want to be able to help him." With Rudy, I noticed he was getting older, and he was in pain sometimes. I knew he didn't like to take medicine, and I tried to find ways to help him feel comfortable. And watching the kittens get sicker and sicker, and there wasn't much to do but keep them comfortable. All those experiences and everything I'm doing in school now have given me the opportunity to learn more so that I can help more.

CHAPTER 9

Caroline and Jamie

It still hurts thinking about Jamie. . . .
My grief is better now. It got better with time.
But I don't think you ever really get over a loss
like that. You just learn to live with it.

— Caroline

Sometimes the animals we fall in love with—and who fall in love with us—weren't ours to begin with. This was Caroline's experience. Her dog Jamie, a Shetland sheepdog, originally belonged to her older sister. "My sister and her boyfriend had broken up," Caroline told me. "She was a teenager, and she was really upset. She wanted a puppy. We made a big joke out of it, like 'I'm going to get a puppy to replace my boyfriend.' So she got Jamie as a comfort. But then she didn't want to take care of a little puppy. She didn't want to stay home and clean up after him, so I did it."

When Jamie came into Caroline's life, her family already had a golden retriever named Misty. Caroline grew up with Misty and loved her, but she was a family dog, while Jamie was all hers. "Jamie and I really bonded," she said. "He was like my baby, like my first little baby. He followed me everywhere. I could just move my hand a certain way, and he'd run right upstairs. He slept with me. At night when we were in bed, I'd give him a handful of water from my water bottle. He was attached to me constantly. We were really close."

It had been many years since Caroline lost her best friend, but her memories of Jamie were still bittersweet and clouded by guilt and regret. Caroline had a lot on her plate when Jamie's health began to fail, and she didn't think she was a very good pet mom. She spoke passionately about the wonderful care provided by the veterinary team at the emergency clinic where Jamie eventually died. For Caroline, redemption lies in offering the same care to other pet keepers and doing everything she can to ensure that animals have a good quality of life.

Caroline

I have so many wonderful memories of Jamie. He was my best friend when I was a kid. When we first got him, he liked playing with our dog Misty. Jamie was so tiny, he'd go underneath Misty, running between her legs. It was hilarious. For Thanksgiving, I used to take a plate, put a tiny bit of everything on it, and give it to him. When he was younger, he used to jump onto a chair, and my mom would always get so mad. She would say, "Get that dog off my table!" And I'd be like, "But he's eating his food. Just let him finish. He'll be done in a minute." He had his own Christmas stocking that we'd put toys and treats into. We still have it. It has a sheltie on it, and I have pictures from the last Christmas we all had together.

I used to play soccer when I was a kid. I played for six years. I'd go outside and play with Jamie all the time. He was really hard to get around, so I practiced my offense with him, even though I'd trip over him a lot. He loved the ball. We always had a little soccer ball for him to chew on. Just the other day, my mom was going through the shed and found this blue soccer ball that I loved. It was all torn up because of all of Jamie's teeth marks, and she said, "Do you want me to throw it out?" And I said, "No. Let's keep it." He would play with me all the time. He was awesome at catching and bouncing the ball. We had a game we played where I'd go to the bottom of the stairs, and I'd toss the ball to him, and he'd hit it back. And if you ever threw a ball in the house, Jamie would come flying out of nowhere, attack the ball, get it in the corner, and just bark at it.

I also took Jamie for training. I was only twelve, and I thought I was so cool because I was going to this training class, and everybody else in the class was an adult. I brought Cheerios for him rather than training treats. That was a lot of fun. That was my first experience really working with an animal. I taught him how to sit and stay, lie down, and roll over. Just basic stuff like that, nothing really advanced. I wanted to do agility, but we never got that far.

But then I started doing bad things when I got into high school. I started smoking, and Jamie would sit outside in the carport with me while I smoked. Sometimes I'd fall asleep out there, and he would stay with me. He wouldn't move. He was just always there. Then I moved out of my parents' house, in and out, in and out. I moved a lot. But whenever I came back, Jamie was always the same. He always loved me, and he always slept with me. I did take him with me a few times during that part of my life. I was living at a hotel with my boyfriend at the time, and I missed Jamie so much. I went home and told my parents that I wanted to take my dog for the night. I fought with them because they weren't happy about it, but I took him to this hotel where dogs weren't allowed. I didn't care. I needed to spend time with my dog no matter what else was going on, and so he stayed with me. I did that a few times over the course of the year when I wasn't living at my parents' house.

But Jamie didn't really like new places. He was hard to travel with because he'd go psycho in the car, barking at everyone. He got really anxious. I didn't like taking him with me a lot. Thinking back on it now, I was caught up in my own life rather than thinking about what was best for him. I feel like a horrible pet mom because I put my needs ahead of his. He was like my baby, and I didn't spend as much time with him as I would have liked. I kept leaving home and living here and there.

Then I moved out West for a while. I was there for a little over a year, and when I came back, I remember walking up to the front door, looking through the window by the door, and seeing Jamie there. I've never seen a dog look shocked before, but Jamie stared at me with this look, as if saying, "Is that really her?" He was so happy that I was home with him again. For a while after I got back, he wouldn't leave me alone, as if he was making sure that I was really going to stay. I was gone only a year or so, but for a dog, that's like forever. I can still picture him sitting by the window, looking at me the way he did.

Maybe six months after I got back, I got pregnant. When my son was born, I was just trying to survive. I couldn't spend as much time with Jamie or give him as much attention as before. I was just exhausted. And that's when he started getting sick. He was just miserable the last few months. He had scabs, and all his hair fell out. I was putting some medicinal wrap around his scabs, and he just looked so sick. It was horrible. They thought he had Cushing's disease because he was constantly peeing, and we had to keep him in the kitchen at night, which upset us both because we were used to sleeping together. I'd always give him treats before I went to bed because I felt bad for him. Then the vet said they thought he had bladder stones, though there was a slight chance he might have cancer.

So my parents were going to take him to the clinic the next morning so they could treat the stones. I had a newborn son, but I needed to be with Jamie. The night before he was going to the vet, I put him in bed with me, one last night. I had this feeling, you know? I had this feeling that something wasn't right. My parents were taking him to the vet early the next morning, and I just didn't think he would come back. I put him in my bed, and that's when I said goodbye to him and told him that I loved him.

Sure enough, when they opened him up at the vet, there was

cancer everywhere. There was nothing we could do for him, so we decided to let him stay at the vet. We were going to go the next day to euthanize him. We were waiting for my sister to get off work, but he died before we got there. I never got to see him again before he died. That really sucked.

Our dog Misty also died of cancer. One afternoon I was petting her, and she had—I don't even know how to describe it—it was like a tumor. It was a bump that had split open, and it was a horrible red color. It looked so painful. I freaked out and called my mom. We took Misty to the vet, and they did an X-ray, and she was just full of tumors. She went downhill so fast. Within a week, she stopped eating, so we decided it was best to euthanize her. But my dad and I couldn't do it because Misty was really close to us. My mom and my older brother took her to the vet to get euthanized, and my dad and I were sobbing and hugging each other in the driveway. That was the only time I ever saw my dad cry.

I didn't really talk to anyone about Misty's death. I was a sophomore in high school when she died, and I didn't have a lot of friends. I just remember not really bringing it up. I mean, in high school you want to fit in because you gotta be cool, right? You don't want to sit there, mope around, and be like, "Oh, my dog died." And people would be like, "It was just a dog. Why are you so upset about it?" That's what I remember about Misty dying. I didn't really mention it to anyone. I just kept on going. With Jamie, it was different. I have a good friend who lives out of state. We've been friends for a long time. We'd dated for a while, and he'd met Jamie. When Jamie died, I texted him and talked about how upset I was. And he was really sad too. That was a comfort.

So I lost two dogs to cancer. It was awful both times. The sickness was awful, and their suffering was awful. I was sad when Misty died because she was my buddy. But with Jamie, I remember feeling like my heart had been ripped out. I went to a counselor who I'd been seeing at the time. I remember talking with her about Jamie's death and about the five stages of grief, trying to figure out how to get through it, because I didn't know what to do. I didn't know how to deal with his death. I kept expecting to see him. He'd always slept in my bed, so it felt really weird when he wasn't there anymore.

After Jamie died, I didn't have time to grieve over the loss. My son was only three months old, and he was really difficult in the first few months. And then there were a lot of other deaths, all within a week or two. My sister's father-in-law died. Then a longtime friend of my parents died too. I felt like I didn't have the time to process any of it, and I don't know that I ever really have.

It still hurts thinking about Jamie, and it makes me sad that I wasn't there enough, that I wasn't better with him. He was like my first baby. I learned a lot about caring for an animal and what it means to be there for them. I think about that now with my son, and I feel bad about it because I didn't always treat Jamie right. My grief is better now. It got better with time. But I don't think you ever really get over a loss like that. You just learn to live with it.

· · ·

From the time I was really little, like three years old, I would go into my dog's house in the backyard. My mom would say, "How can you go in there?" I have no sense of smell whatsoever, and I guess I never did because the smell never bothered me. I've always been happiest when I'm around dogs. I've had dogs all my life. I can't imagine not having one. Dogs have always made me happy. They've always been there for me and comforted me. They don't talk back to you. They're not mean to you like people are. I knew I could always count on dogs, and in my work, I want to help dogs especially.

I want to work in a small-animal practice and maybe at an emergency vet clinic. Both my dogs died so suddenly of cancer. Toward the end of Jamie's life, I had to take him to the emergency vet. He wasn't doing well, and they were just so nice there. I remember thinking, "What would I have done if you guys weren't here?" I would have had to stay up the entire night to make sure something horrible didn't happen.

They asked me if I wanted to leave him there overnight. I was very pregnant, but I said, "I can stay up. I can do it. I can spend the whole night with him." My mom said, "You really shouldn't do that." She was right, I think, because I was having some trouble with my pregnancy, and I was so relieved that the people at the emergency clinic were able to help him and monitor him all night.

I've loved all my animals, but my connection with Jamie was different. It was just special. To have somebody look after him who wasn't me, I just couldn't imagine it. But I was so pregnant and so tired, and I was afraid I was going to fall asleep, and he was going to die. Oh my god. Leaving him with the vet was the best thing. I trusted them. And that's what I want to do for people. I was so distraught, and they were so nice. When I picture myself in that role, I think how awesome it would be to help somebody like that. I will take care of your pet. They are important to me too. I know what it's like to lose a pet, and it is not fun, so I will do everything I can to help your animal because you want someone to care about you and what you care about. And to be honest, I hadn't really made that connection until now—the connection between my experience with Jamie and what I want to do with my life.

CHAPTER 10

Colleen and Pretzel

*I think people are becoming more and more attached
to their animals. They care more so they want us
to care more. What is going to make or break the
veterinary world is this genuine care.*

— Colleen

Colleen was an outspoken, no-nonsense young woman who shared the story of her childhood dog, a long-haired dachshund named Pretzel. Her memories of Pretzel were both joyful and troubled—joyful because of her happy memories of their good times together and troubled because she lost him again and again when he was shuffled between households after her parents' divorce.

Colleen was a teenager living with her mom when Pretzel's health began to decline. Pretzel was eventually euthanized, and Colleen's recollection of his death offers insight into the many challenges of purposely ending a pet's life. Her story shows that our pets are deeply enmeshed in our families and that people bring their history with them when they walk into a veterinary clinic, including all their personal struggles. It also shows that getting a hug when we need it can make a huge difference in our ability to cope with losing a pet.

Colleen's story also teaches us that one way we cope with a difficult loss is by trying to right the wrongs we've experienced or witnessed. Colleen was distressed by Pretzel's death, but no one in the veterinary clinic where Pretzel was euthanized reached out to help her. That event has shaped her determination to provide genuine, loving care for her clients in her work as a vet tech. She understands that caring is as important as curing when it comes to pets, and this was a hard-earned insight. I have no doubt she'll provide the warm hugs and kind words she didn't receive herself when she lost her friend Pretzel.

Colleen

I got Pretzel when I was eight years old. He was my dog, and my dad let me name him. I named him Pretzel because he was a wiener dog.

Pretzel and I had a good relationship. As a kid, I took him everywhere. My dad, brother, and I went fishing a lot. We also went mushroom hunting, and Pretzel was always with us. He went on every car ride. If we went to Walmart, he'd go with us. There wasn't really a time when he didn't go with us, even when he wasn't allowed. We used to sneak him into hotels because he was so small that no one knew he was there. Going on beach trips wasn't a problem because we'd just sneak him in. He'd start barking sometimes, but we'd be like, "Pretzel, be quiet! Shhh." And he'd stop.

One of my best memories is riding my bike with Pretzel. I would pick him up, put him on the handlebars, and hold his little feet. We'd ride around the neighborhood, and everyone would laugh because he was so cute. He loved it. He didn't want to get down. I have an older brother, but he's a lot older than me. I never had a little brother or sister to play with, so Pretzel was all I had. That's why I used to dress him up in baby doll clothes and paint his nails. He was like my little brother. He was my baby.

Pretzel was different than most dogs. Some people just get a dog and say, "Oh, that's my family dog," while the dog is over there drooling or licking himself. But Pretzel knew tricks, and he liked people. You could say, "Oh look, Pretzel, Mama's almost home. Let's run to the door." He'd get so excited; he couldn't wait for Mama to get home. We actually trained him. We made him a part of our family.

But then everything fell apart, and my mom and dad split. My dad and brother moved out West, and my mom and I moved to the East Coast. I remember packing up the U-Haul and driving away. Pretzel came with me and my mom. But then my mom had to work four to midnight, so it was just me and Pretzel every night. I had to go to school during the day, so Pretzel was left at home by himself a lot. He was used to being with us all the time, so he went from always being with us to having nobody. It was the same for me. We both went from having a family, coming home to people, dinners, carrying on, singing, all this different stuff, to nothing.

He started acting out. We had to put a muzzle on him so he wouldn't bark because my mom and I lived in an apartment. Then he tore the carpet, trying to get out the door to go with us, so we had to pay for the carpet. We didn't have any money. My mom told me Pretzel needed to go with my dad and brother out West, thousands of miles away. So they came and took him away. Pretzel was supposed to be my dog, but he became my dad's dog. My mom said he would be better off going with my dad and brother because he was just happier with my dad.

I didn't see Pretzel for at least a year or two. I moved here for middle school. I was in sixth grade for half a year at one school, then we moved again, and I finished sixth grade at another school. I went to seventh grade at yet another school, and then my brother, my dog, and my dad came back to live with us again. They were in and out of my life for a while. We all stayed together for a little bit because I remember living in a house instead of an apartment. So I got Pretzel back for a little while, but it didn't last—maybe not even a year. Then my dad and brother left again, and my mom and I were alone again in a big house, but my mom couldn't afford it, which forced us to move. Again. When my brother and my dad left us the second time, they took Pretzel with them.

• • •

Pretzel came back to me many years later. I was in eleventh grade, so it was like five or six years since I had seen him. Things weren't so great for me and my dad. I was really pissed off at him. I told my brother that if my dad didn't want to come for my high school graduation, he could just kiss me goodbye from his life because I obviously hadn't been on his priority list. I'd tried to contact my dad, but he wouldn't talk to me. He'd pass me off to someone else, or he'd always be at a bar. I'd have to call and try to find him. I'd have to hunt him down just to talk to him. He never once called me. I got to that breaking point where I didn't care anymore. I told my brother, "If Dad doesn't come to my graduation, that's it," and I told him that he was more of a father figure to me than Dad was. My brother basically forced my dad to come back, and it wasn't long after that that Pretzel passed away.

We found out that Pretzel wasn't doing well when he stopped eating. He wouldn't even eat wet food anymore, and he'd always loved wet food. We could stick steak in front of his face, and he wouldn't move. He didn't care. He didn't want to get up to use the bathroom. He didn't even care if we walked in the door anymore. It was getting to the point where he looked like he wanted to die. He was looking rough, just skin and bones. You could see his ribs because he was so sick. We took him to the doctor when he started getting sick, but we didn't have any money. My family doesn't have lots of money. My sister was doing a lot better at that time, so she paid the veterinarian to figure out what was wrong with Pretzel. It was kidney failure. The vet said it was going to be in the thousands to fix him, and my sister immediately said, "No, I can't give you that much. I can't help you." The vet said our only other option was to euthanize him because it's inhumane to keep him alive when he's basically dying. He would have died eventually, maybe within the next few days, because he wasn't eating, and he wasn't himself anymore.

We really had no choice but to euthanize him, and it sucked because not everybody could be there. I was a junior in high school, and my family and I had been back and forth, together, apart, together, apart. My mom couldn't be there. She had to go to work because bills don't stop coming in. That left only my brother and me to take Pretzel to the vet for his euthanasia, and we didn't have a car, so I had to call a friend to give us a ride. [crying]

The vet said the euthanasia was going to be painless, but it wasn't. When they injected the drugs, Pretzel was huffing. He was trying to catch his breath, and he couldn't. My brother and I witnessed that, and my brother got really pissed. He was like, "You told me this was going to be painless. It wasn't painless. I can't take this." He walked out and left me in the room with some girl who worked there, like a vet assistant. She was just staring at me. She didn't try to comfort me. She just said, "Do you want to be alone with him?" I said no. Because I didn't want to be alone with him. I didn't want that to be my last memory of Pretzel, watching him struggle to breathe. It was my first death. It was the first death I'd had in my whole life.

I didn't think it was going to be like that. I didn't think I was going to literally hear my dog gasp for his last breath before he passed. I didn't think I would witness that. I just wanted to be there for my dog. I didn't want to give him away to some strange people and then have him killed without us being there. I felt like we at least owed him that. I tried to stay with him, but I couldn't because my brother left me, and I didn't want to be there alone with him. It still hurts so much. [crying]

I remember hovering over him and trying to give him a hug. Then I just left. It was a quiet car ride back home.

We never really talked about it, I guess because that's how my family is. We don't talk about our feelings, and my sister didn't really seem to care. I don't want to say it like that, but she really didn't show that she cared. We got Pretzel after she left for college, and she wasn't around him as much as my brother, mom, dad, and I were. She only saw him every now and again, which is probably why her attachment to him wasn't as great as mine.

In my life, I've always been by myself. It's sad to say, but I've closed myself off from people. I don't know how to express my feelings, and I don't think people care when I talk. So I was alone a lot. When I first moved East with my mom, she was working a late shift, so I hardly saw her. I didn't have friends. I was a tomboy, and I wore baggy clothes. I didn't have mall-designer clothes. Everyone made fun of me because I was from the country, and I had never lived in a city before. I didn't know what I had gotten myself into, but I had to go to school. For a while, I didn't really have people to talk to. My sister was here, and she let us stay in her apartment because we didn't have any money. She moved in with her boyfriend, who is now her husband. My mom and I basically lived in her apartment so we wouldn't be homeless. My sister did that for us, so I'm thankful for that.

I've had some friends pass away since I lost Pretzel. A friend I was really close with was twenty-one when he passed away last year. Two kids hit a tree, and the car blew up and they died. Those were my friends. I went to the cemetery the other night to put flowers by their graves, but it really didn't hit home. I couldn't cry. I tried to cry. I mean, I cried a little bit, but I couldn't really grieve. Pretzel's death is the only one that ever really hit home. Everything else since then, I was just numb. I guess I'm used to the pain.

· · ·

When I think about Pretzel, I try not to think about the negative things that happened because there are always going to be negative things. I don't like to think about how awful it was the way he died. I can't change that. But I can definitely change how I see it. I don't have to see him as I last saw him. I have it in my head, and I can't erase it, but I choose not to see him that way.

Thank god I have my dog, Sidney. She helps me. She's also a dachshund, and when I see her, I think about Pretzel. I think about how he was in life, not death, and that helps a lot. Sidney reminds me of him. She has a very similar face, and her ears flop down, just like Pretzel's. When she acts like Pretzel, it helps me keep him alive in my heart because they're just so similar. She reminds me so much of him that it makes me smile. It's a way for him to live here with us still. So even though Pretzel is not actually here, we can keep him alive in our memories.

Sidney is my baby. I got her when I graduated from high school. I asked my mom as a joke if she would let me have her. I thought she was going to say no, but she said yes. I got her about a year after Pretzel passed. She was eight and a half weeks old. I basically saved her because I had to go to the middle of nowhere to pick her up. Her coat is tan, but when I got her, she was black—absolutely covered in dirt or soot or something. You couldn't see the gold and white in her coat. Sidney had fleas all over her, and when the lady handed her to me, she peed all over me because she was terrified. And then when I took her home, she drooled, and I mean, *drooled*, like major salivation. Because of my vet tech schooling, I know now that Sidney drooled so much because she was in shock. I had just come and taken her away. I was a complete stranger.

I let her sleep in my bed with me to make her feel more comfortable. I made a little bed for her next to my head, on my pillow, and she slept there on a towel. Well, the next day I woke up and, frickin', the dog had worms. I was literally sleeping with worms because they were everywhere. They were crawling all over my bed. When we took her outside, they would fall out of her butt. It was gross. It was nasty. And I'm like, "Am I really going to keep this dog?" That's what I was thinking. I told my friends, "I don't think I'm going to keep this dog," and I told my family, "I don't think I want this dog anymore." Because, number one, she was scared of me, and, number two, she had all this stuff wrong with her, and not just the physical stuff. She was terrified of people. She didn't want to come near people. She would sit in a corner and just shake. I would give her a treat—bones, wet food, stuff dogs go crazy for—and she just wouldn't move.

But every day, I just picked her up and loved on her. It was summer when I got her, but when the weather got colder, I'd put her in my jacket, and she'd go right to sleep because she was a puppy, and all she wanted to do was sleep. So Sidney and I got closer and closer, and she finally opened up to me. Now she's my dog, and she's great. I don't know what made her open up. She just did. I remember thinking, "You're going to love me, and I'm going to love you, and we're going to make this work." I would hold her and cradle her. I took some pictures of us this morning. She cuddles with me like a baby. She's just like a baby. She'll let me do whatever to her because she trusts me. I can hold her upside down. She is completely and totally happy with anything I do.

Sidney is just like Pretzel. She knows so many tricks. I can make her climb up and down a ladder to get to me. She will run in a lake to get to me. She will go in the ocean. It was the same way with Pretzel. Once those dogs hit sand? They both turned into different dogs. Pretzel and Sidney would both start digging, digging, digging, trying to find something, like there's a hidden treasure. They would run off and run right back and run circles around us, but they would never run away from us. They were just so happy to be at the beach. Pretzel would sit in a beach chair. We'd wrap him in a towel, and he'd just watch us. Now Sidney does the same thing. She likes to sit on her butt, like a person, with her feet sticking straight out. We call it "just chilling." [laughs]

All my friends and family she's grown up with—she recognizes all these different people. If she sees my friend Candace who's in a wheelchair, Sidney immediately jumps right up onto her lap, and licks her, and we're like, "Sidney got you!" Sidney just brings joy to my life.

• • •

In my veterinary classes, they say that euthanasia is painless, but I don't agree with that. I really don't. Because the way I saw Pretzel die? It was just unacceptable. I would rather have let him die the way he was. I wonder sometimes if he knew we'd killed him, you know, my brother and I, the people who loved him. Did he know that we killed him?

In school, they kill lab rats so we can see what a necropsy looks like. But to kill a living being just to watch it die? That's not OK with me. I guess to some people it's just a mouse, but every living thing feels. I just care a lot about animals. I always have. Everybody has their purpose in life, and I want to fulfill mine, and I feel like that purpose is to help animals. Ever since I was a kid, I've always had a care for animals. I wanted to take them in and care for them. I guess I'm a softy. I mean, I cried when my betta fish died, and they only live like a year or so.

If someone were going through something similar to what we went through with Pretzel, I know I can be there to comfort them. It's OK to put your arm around someone, to give them a hug if they need it. That's what I needed and what I didn't get. My dog had just died in front of me, and this girl was just sitting there staring at me like, "Do you want me to leave you alone with your dead dog that we just euthanized in front of you and huffed his last breath?" To me, that's when she should have stepped in and been like, "I'm a human. I have feelings too. I can see that you're hurting here and that you might need my hand or a hug. Would you like a hug?" She could have said that, and I would have stayed longer and spent the extra time I needed with Pretzel. It didn't seem like the vet really cared much. Pretzel was just another dog to them. And that's why people get so upset with veterinarians and technicians, because they really do make it seem like it's all about money sometimes.

In my work, I want to be on a different level. I really do care. I want to comfort people because I know what they're going through. I know it's not easy. For me and my brother, it's not like we had people to turn to. Like I said, our family didn't talk about emotions. I think the vet is the place to talk about those things for some people. Some clinics have consultation rooms. I didn't get taken into a consultation room when Pretzel was euthanized. No one talked to me about my dog's euthanasia or how it was going to be or how some animals have bad reactions. I was only told it would be painless, so that's what I expected. But I know it wasn't painless for him, and it makes me angry to this day. It's all in how you word it. You have to be honest with people and tell them what actually happens during euthanasia.

Personally, I want to know that the people who look after my dog really care about my dog and care about me too. And I don't mean care as in medical care. I want to know how much *you* care. Do you care about me? Do you care about my pet? If you don't have that connection with someone, they're not going to come back to your clinic. The most important thing is the relationship you build with the pet and the client. I think people are becoming more and more attached to their animals. *They* care more, so they want *us* to care more. What is going to make or break the veterinary world is this genuine care.

What helps me now in my studies as a vet tech
is that I draw on my experience with Freddie. I've
grown so much because of him. I have more empathy
and compassion for people and their animals, and I
cope better with stress and loss.

— Lillian

CHAPTER 11

Lillian and Freddie

I met Lillian, a woman in her mid- to late-thirties, on a clear winter day at a local coffee shop near my home. She was friendly and animated and talked passionately about her relationship with Freddie, a beautiful Maine coon she'd adopted from a rescue when she was a young woman starting out on her own.

Lillian had grown up on a farm and kept many pets throughout her life. But Freddie was unique. Her relationship with him was different from any she'd enjoyed before. Her experiences with Freddie changed her perspective on the human-animal bond, deepening her appreciation for the powerful connection many people share with their animal companions.

Lillian's journey of grief after Freddie died was long and difficult. It was truly a journey—a "process," as she called it—that entailed the slow transformation of her emotions and worldview. At the time of the interview, it had been three years since Freddie had died, and her sorrow for his loss was still sharp, though it was no longer the deep, heart-stopping pain she'd felt when he was euthanized. She felt terrible guilt for that decision, and she was in a daze in the weeks following his death, as if she were merely going through the motions of daily life without being fully present. Life no longer held meaning without Freddie, and a great emptiness opened in her heart.

In response to this mix of guilt, sorrow, and meaninglessness, Lillian threw herself into her schoolwork and animal rescue, in part as a way of distracting herself from her grief. She eventually learned to live with her grief and allow her feelings of sadness and guilt to come and go rather than trying to ignore them. She tended to her grief, but she wasn't grief's captive. As the days passed and she focused on her work, her path began to shift. The sorrow and emptiness she felt began to recede while a new sense of meaning and purpose emerged.

Lillian's story about Freddie is a thoughtful, honest reflection on the journey of grief for a cherished animal companion. Love changes us, and so does death. Sometimes, we might become wiser, more compassionate people.

Lillian

My cat's name was Frederick, but I called him Freddie. I adopted him from a shelter in my town. I was not expecting to get a cat that day. In fact, it was the last thing on my mind. I was just dropping off my recycling, and something told me to go into the shelter. And that's when I saw Freddie. Our eyes met, and it was like he called to me. I can't explain it. He was the only cat I looked at that day. He was a huge

Maine coon, just absolutely beautiful. I took him out of his cage, and I filled out the application form that day. I cursed them for not letting me take him home right away. I thought about him all the time while I was waiting because he was my cat, right from the start. I think we were meant to be together. It was an immediate bond.

Freddie was my constant companion for sixteen years. Everybody knew he was everything to me. Not every cat could be like that, and I've never had that type of relationship with a cat. I've had many, many cats. I've had barn cats. I had cats growing up on my parents' farm. But I never had that type of relationship with a cat. He slept in my bed. He hung out on the couch with me. We studied together. We read together. We did everything together. He was like my baby. To say I loved him doesn't quite capture what I felt for him. I can only say it was a different kind of love than I'd experienced before.

When Freddie became sick, I became sick too. I stopped sleeping. I stood vigil by him. I made a bed in the corner of my apartment and stayed by him. I had to make the decision to euthanize him. It was the hardest decision. I remember for days I just couldn't bring myself to end his life. Days went by, and I don't think he was ready to go, and I wasn't ready to let him go. But then one day, he told me he was tired and was ready. It wasn't like he spoke to me, but I knew that cat so well, and I knew he was ready. It was normal for him to lie on my stomach when we sat on the couch together, but then that changed. His breathing changed too.

So I called the vet, and I don't know how I got the words out, but I told them it was time. They were very kind. They said it was the right decision. Because it was—any kind of treatment was only prolonging his life and quite possibly putting him in more pain, and I didn't want that. For sixteen years, he had given me unconditional love. He'd given me so much, and he deserved unconditional love back. He deserved that gift. [crying]

So I took him to the vet, and I held him. I said goodbye, and he went so very quickly. The vet tech took him away because I had made the decision to cremate him. Thank goodness I had previously made all the arrangements with them because at that time I wasn't sane. I felt like I was floating on air. I was in such a state of shock that the vet tech escorted me out of the office, as if I were a porcelain doll. That's how I felt—so fragile, as if I could break into a million pieces if I bumped into a piece of furniture.

When we came into the waiting room, there was this crazy lady there. Now, I shouldn't call her crazy. She had a cat in a pink baby carriage, and when she saw me, she asked what was wrong. But I couldn't even talk. I think I just stared at her and the pink baby carriage. I remember those details, but I think I was in shock because it was like being in a dream. The vet tech who was with me told the woman everything was OK, then she took me by the hand and walked me to my car. She put me in the car and asked, "Can you drive?" And I said, "Yes." And then she said, "Call me as soon as you get back." I was so grateful to that tech because to her it wasn't just another procedure on another animal, like putting a catheter in for a urinalysis or whatever. She cared about Freddie, and she also cared about me. She cared about that lady too, the one with the cat in the pink baby carriage. I'll never stop going to that vet because I knew they cared about Freddie, and because they cared about Freddie, I knew they cared about me too.

• • •

After Freddie died, I had a hard time coping. At the time of his death, I was very grateful to my vet and the vet techs. They were very helpful. I talked to them about how sad I was. But I don't remember speaking a lot about him to friends. People knew that he had passed. My friends would ask me how I was doing, and I would say, "Oh, it's OK." I think I wasn't ready to talk about losing him. And some people blew it off. I had one friend who said, "Oh, it was just a cat." And that's when I shut down, like, "OK, we're not talking about this."

I was offended at first, like "Oh, how dare you?" It's not fair, you know, because Freddie was more than a cat. He was a very special cat.

My relationship with Freddie changed my perspective on the love that can happen between a person and an animal. I grew up on a farm and had been around animals all my life, but Freddie helped me see animals differently. He helped me respect the bond in a new way. When people say they have that bond with their dog or their cat or their bird or their snake or their turtle, I understand it differently now because I experienced that with Freddie.

Later, I interpreted that kind of comment differently. I thought, "Well, you know, people who say things like 'Oh, it was just a dog or a cat' or whatever have never had that bond with an animal. And that's a shame. It's the same as somebody never knowing love, and that's a terrible thing."

I reached out to my mother when Freddie died. She has dogs she's close to, and she was supportive, but there wasn't much she could say that seemed to help. But I knew she understood how much I loved Freddie. Normally, when people visit their parents, they leave the cat at home and have somebody feed the cat. But I would always pack Freddie up and bring him with me, even if it was just for one night. Freddie was just part of my life like that. So my mom saw that I had a special bond with him and that he was a special cat. I think she loved Freddie, and I think she grieved when he died, though she won't admit it. My father was sad too. We raised chickens, goats, llamas, and horses. For my dad, Freddie wasn't just another farm animal, and I think he was sad when Freddie died, even though we didn't talk about it much.

I've talked about Freddie with some of the people I've met in the rescue where I work. Not in a lot of detail. Just a little bit. But a lot of people who do rescue, they almost always have had or still have a very close bond with an animal. They know what it's like to lose one you're really close to. They understand what it is to be bonded with a cat. We all wear that "crazy cat lady" title with pride. [laughs] So I didn't actually have to talk about Freddie's death very much to know they understood what that was like for me.

. . .

When I first lost Freddie, I threw myself into my schoolwork. It was a way of coping. And then I really got into meditation and yoga. But I was just going through the motions. I think staying busy was a form of denial because I wasn't really processing my grief. I was just covering it up with all this activity. But underneath I was just sad all the time. I learned there's a difference between being in a moment of sadness, in a particular place or time, and just being deeply, always sad. I had to learn to be OK with that. I had to accept my sadness and not try to pretend I didn't feel it. I also had to get over the guilt, because sometimes I felt like I was a bad person because I wanted to be happy and move forward.

Initially, working in rescue was a way of avoiding my grief. But then, with time, my work became Freddie's legacy because Freddie was a rescue. I know I can't save them all, but the more energy I put into helping other animals, the more this work becomes Freddie's legacy. My work in rescue is how he lives on, and that's because with each life I save, a little piece of his spirit lives on. His life had value. That's the place I eventually came to, and I found peace in that.

I also work in rescue because I want everyone else to feel the bond like I felt with Freddie. It was just so special. Even the cats I have now, the ones I've rescued and the ones I'm fostering, the bond is not the same. I'm always striving to find that kind of love in the world, the kind of love that I experienced with Freddie, and I think everyone should have that love.

My relationship with Freddie helped me better understand the human-animal bond. I raised him from when he was a kitten all through his life and his death, and I was with him for everything. If you've never had that bond, you don't really understand when people refer to their dog as their baby or have cute, affectionate nicknames for their pets, or maybe you have a little less patience for somebody who puts their cat in a baby carriage. It's a little too much. OK, I admit it, the cat probably doesn't like it. But once you understand the bond, you have a little more patience with people who do things like that. The truth is that pet care is a multi-billion-dollar industry. People go crazy for their pets, and it's a big deal for them. The human-animal bond is a big deal, and you have to respect it and not just like, "OK, I respect your opinion, so it's OK, you just be you." You have to really understand how bonded people are with their animals, and you have to communicate that you understand where they're coming from.

You also have to be careful not to judge people for the choices they make about their animals. In one of my classes, we talked about euthanasia, and some of the students were very vocal about the fact that they didn't approve of euthanasia. One student thought that cremation was "gross." Well, I'd euthanized Freddie and had him cremated because I wanted him close to me. I didn't want to bury him on my parents' farm. So when that student made that comment about cremation, I felt judged, and I never talked about Freddie with the other students. But that experience also encouraged me to respect other people's wishes for their animals. I don't care if somebody decides to taxidermy their dog because it's their personal decision. It's their dog, cat, bat, or turtle. It's not my place to judge them because I know what that feels like, and it doesn't feel good.

Grieving was definitely a process. It took time. It didn't happen overnight. When I say a process, I think I'm still going through it, and Freddie died three years ago. [laughs] What helps me now in my studies as a vet tech is that I draw on my experience with Freddie. I've grown so much because of Freddie. I have more empathy and compassion for people and their animals. I also cope better with stress and loss.

I still think about Freddie and the bond we shared. I miss him. I miss hugging him because he was my huggy bear. Not having him with me still hurts, although the terrible pain of losing him is pretty much gone. Now it's just love. I still have his pictures up. I just moved, and I was unpacking things this weekend, and that was one of the first things that went up on the bookshelf—Freddie's picture. I still love Freddie, and I always will.

Discussion Questions

1. Of the stories presented in the last ten chapters, select two that you identify with or in which you feel some kinship with the storyteller. Describe why these stories resonate with you and any personal experiences they bring to mind.

2. Select two stories you don't relate to or in which you struggle to identify with the storyteller. Describe why these stories are hard to relate to and any personal experiences they bring to mind.

3. What did you learn from reading these stories? Describe your top three takeaways.

A Spiritual Journey
Through Pet Keeping and Loss

CHAPTER 12

The Healing Power of Storytelling

The stories presented in the last ten chapters offer great insight into the unique experience of loving and losing an animal companion. As noted in the introduction, they're all *sacred stories*, or those narratives that speak to the storytellers' deeply held values and beliefs and their sense of meaning and purpose.

In reading these stories, I hope you were inspired to reflect on your own experiences with pets. This is the power of storytelling. When we bear witness to others' experiences through their stories—especially when those stories are shared with vulnerability and authenticity—we may be inspired to call forth our own stories. In this way, our stories connect us, helping us bridge our differences and discover our commonalities. We all benefit, and as a veterinary chaplain, my goal is to create safe spaces where pet keepers can share their stories with each other and provide mutual support.

I've witnessed the healing power of storytelling throughout my service as a veterinary chaplain. I'm confident, for example, that the vet tech students I spoke with benefitted from their interviews with me. Some had never had the opportunity to discuss their heart animals at length with someone who was curious and nonjudgmental. In addition to my official researcher's hat, I privately wore my chaplain's hat during the interviews, frequently using communication techniques that I rely on in my caregiving work. My chaplaincy skills were instrumental in helping me build rapport with the students and gain their trust. All the students thanked me for the opportunity to talk about their pets. Some told me the interviews were revelatory and gave them new insight into the connection between their experiences with their heart animals, their family and friends, and their interest in veterinary medicine.

In today's media-rich world, authentic stories like these can be hard to find. When you think about stories, you might think about entertainment: the social media posts, books, videos, movies, plays, and other mediums that carry our words and images out into the world. Yet for human beings, stories are far more than entertainment. They reveal who we are as individuals and as a community. They reveal what's important to us, what we aspire to, and the legacy we hope to leave behind. Telling stories is innate to human beings because it's the primary way we make sense of the world and create ourselves. American writer Patrick Rothfuss observes, "It's like everyone tells a story about themselves inside their own head. Always. All the time. That story makes you what you are. We build ourselves out of that story."[1]

Our stories are also one of the most meaningful ways we connect with others. In telling our stories, we share our most authentic selves and strengthen our connection with the people who receive them. This is especially important when we're navigating stressful situations, including the loss of a loved one. Clinical psychologist Janice Nadeau studied bereaved families who had lost a human family member to determine how they coped with their loss.[2] She found that the most common strategy for making meaning of loss was through storytelling. Sharing our stories about a deceased loved one can be cathartic and help us make sense of a life-changing loss.

The point is that storytelling is both a defining characteristic of human nature and an important way to cope with the loss of a loved one. So what happens to people who cannot share their stories with others?

This is precisely the quandary in which many pet keepers find themselves after losing an animal companion. Research has shown that three-quarters of US pet keepers grieve alone and avoid sharing their story about their pet with anyone because they worry that others won't understand their anguish and they might be judged for grieving intensely for an animal.[3] Such isolation compounds our sorrow. When we're unable to share our vital stories, we may lack satisfying and meaningful connections with others. As educator Mary Rose O'Reilley notes in the book *Radical Presence,* "If one is aware of storytelling as a way of being present in the world, one soon becomes aware of its opposite: not telling. If we can't tell our story, if it's caught in our throats, it seems to block our spirit's longing to participate in the world. At an extreme, we can't reach out at all."[4]

Many animal lovers have stories caught in their throats. Some have never shared their stories about their pets with anyone. One particularly troubling phenomenon I've encountered concerns people who lost pets as children but were never given the opportunity to talk about their grief. Sometimes animals simply disappeared with no explanation, or a parent told them their pet went to a better home or a happier place. I've also heard painful stories of the violent deaths, abuse, neglect, and abandonment of pets that people witnessed when they were children. Such experiences can be terribly upsetting, and for most people they remain unexplored.

As I've said, my mission as a veterinary chaplain is to liberate people's stories about their pets, and I developed the Pet Chaplain Learning Series to achieve this goal. As noted in the introduction, the first three books in the learning series offer a spiritual journey in which you'll explore your connection with animals and tell your sacred story about the pets who've changed your life. We'll begin this journey in the next chapter with a discussion of human spirituality. To appreciate the contours of the journey ahead—or the landscape in which we'll be traveling, so to speak—we must first understand what spirituality is and how we experience and express it.

CHAPTER 13

Defining Human Spirituality

We often talk casually about spirituality without giving much thought to the meaning of this common term. Because spirituality can mean different things to different people, it's difficult to define. Yet it's a critical aspect of the human condition. The way we conceive of spirituality influences many aspects of our lives, including our beliefs about animals and how we interact with them, our social interactions with other people and the communities that develop around a shared worldview, and how we cope with losing a loved one.

So what is human spirituality? First, it's important to acknowledge that spirituality is not synonymous with religion, though religion is one way that many people express their spirituality. Religion is an organized or institutionalized system of beliefs and practices that concern a divine power or form, such as the monolithic God of the Abrahamic religious traditions or the many gods and goddesses of Hinduism and paganism. Religious traditions also typically include written doctrines concerning the nature of the divine and norms that regulate our behavior. In contrast, spirituality tends to be much less organized than religion. It's highly personal and concerns the way we frame our place in our communities, the world, and the cosmos.

In *Exploring Spirituality and Culture in Adult and Higher Education,*

Elizabeth J. Tisdell examines how people in contemporary Western Society think about spirituality.[1] Tisdell is a professor of adult education, and her goal is to understand how people acquire new knowledge and how professionals in adult and higher education can encourage spiritual development in the classroom. As an adult educator, I share her goal, and I also find her discussion of spirituality refreshingly free of religious ideology.

Tisdell identifies three primary themes of spirituality: first, the abiding sense that all things are connected and, for many people, the belief that a higher power beyond our comprehension is at work in the universe; second, the way we make meaning of our experiences; and third, the ongoing movement toward an authentic spiritual identity. Each of these themes is addressed in the learning series. In this chapter, I'll briefly describe these themes and the various ways we express our spirituality.

Interconnection

Tisdell writes that "spirituality is about an awareness and honoring of wholeness and the interconnectedness of all things through the mystery of what many refer to as the Life-force, God, higher power, higher self, cosmic energy, Buddha nature, or Great Spirit."[2] Within this broad category, people might express their spirituality through participation in religious institutions that offer robust, comprehensive understandings of how the cosmos is organized and our connection to the divine. Someone who follows an ancient Indigenous spiritual practice might believe that all things, including inanimate objects, contain a spiritual essence.

In contrast, people who identify as humanist or atheist might understand the interconnectedness of things through a scientific lens, and many experience a powerful sense of awe and wonder as they contemplate the complexity of the natural world. Many people also blend spiritual traditions with scientific understandings of the world.

All these expressions are equally valid, and we must be cautious in assuming that only someone who participates in a religious tradition is spiritual, while someone who doesn't attend religious services or believe in the existence of a divine being is not.

Spirituality is about deep connection—with each other, animals, all life, and the earth itself, the cosmos, and stardust of which all life is composed, and with the divine, however you may conceive of it. Our spirituality is found in the awe, wonder, and gratitude we feel when we become aware of these connections. It resides comfortably with the mysteries of life and death, and it is readily apparent in the profound sense of love and connection we enjoy with our heart animals.

While spirituality is about connection, it also concerns wholeness. Notably, the words *wholeness*, *holiness*, and *health* all have the same root word, *hal*, which is Old Saxon for *health*.[3] The spiritual journey you'll undertake with the learning series is one that moves toward wholeness, holiness, and health. Such goals are fundamentally what spirituality is all about.

Meaning-Making

In addition to our sense that all things are interconnected, Tisdell asserts that spirituality is "fundamentally about how we make meaning in our lives, particularly with regard to our overall life purpose. . . . Individuals do what they feel called to do—what gives their lives meaning."[4]

This aspect of spirituality is readily apparent in the stories in this book, which all concern a calling the vet tech students felt to care for animals and the people who love them. Celeste spoke eloquently about her calling when she said, "I think I was put on the earth like St. Francis or Noah or somebody like that, where I think my whole job on Earth is to help the animals. And that's it. That's all I'm here for." Colleen shared a similar sentiment when she said, "Everybody has their purpose in life, and I want to fulfill mine, and I feel like that purpose is to help animals."

Meaning-making or *meaning-seeking* are not terms most of us are familiar with, but we all make meaning of our experiences, from the most mundane occurrences to the life-changing events that we never forget. We do this primarily through storytelling. Our stories encompass all aspects of our lives—who we are, what we value, and how we believe the world works. When life unfolds as we believe it should—when all is going according to plan—we feel good about who we are and what we hold to be true and sacred. But when life doesn't unfold as expected or something happens that challenges our worldview, we may feel lost, and our lives may become devoid of meaning and purpose. The loss of a pet can be precisely this—a life-changing experience that compels each of us to reframe our identity, values, and worldview. Fortunately, our most pivotal experiences may also be joyful, as when we encounter a heart animal who shifts our perspective about animals and deepens our appreciation for their unique gifts. The bottom line is that spirituality always involves meaning-making.

Discovering Our Authentic Selves

Tisdell defines this aspect of spirituality as "having a sense that one is operating more from a sense of self that is defined by one's own self as opposed to being defined by other people's expectations." For many of us, spiritual authenticity means living in a way that honors our deeply held values. In turn, spiritual development is a continual process of moving closer to this authentic self through new learning and critical self-reflection.

For people who believe in an all-powerful God, the authentic self is generally equated with the immortal soul, or an essence that is God-given and partakes of God's divine spirit. For Buddhists, the equivalent of this authentic self is known as the "Buddha nature." However it is framed, it's important to understand that discovering our authentic selves is a lifelong process. It's a challenging journey. Even if we don't always make decisions in keeping with our authentic selves, we can nonetheless strive to attain spiritual authenticity by making choices and engaging in work that is personally meaningful and consistent with our values and beliefs.

The learning series offers you the opportunity to better understand your authentic identity as a pet keeper, animal lover, animal protector and healer, or however you might describe yourself. Through new learning, self-reflection, and storytelling, you'll explore your past, connect it with your present, and envision where you might want to go in the future as you continue to explore your relationships with your fellow human beings, other animals, and the greater-than-human world. What do you believe about animals, spirituality, and the cosmos? What are our ethical obligations to the animals in our midst? If you feel called to help and protect animals—or to support people who are grieving the loss of animals—how can you make that calling a reality? You'll engage with these questions and others like them throughout this journey.

How We Express Our Spirituality

Within the three broad themes we just reviewed—interconnection, meaning-making, and discovering our authentic selves—we may express our spirituality in diverse ways. As Tisdell observes, many people have "significant spiritual experiences relating to particular milestones in their identity development or other important aspects of their life experiences, such as understanding their life purpose, dealing with the death of a loved one or working through some other painful life experience, or celebrating some special joy."[5] Therapist Pamela A. Hays refers to such events as "shimmering moments."[6] What Hays is naming here is a rare glimpse into the interconnectedness of things. They occur when our most intimate thoughts and feelings converge with ultimate meanings, when finite experience meets infinite reality.

We often consider these moments to be sacred. Shimmering moments may become lifelong touchpoints we return to again and again. They guide and inform us as we reflect on new experiences through the lens of ultimate meanings, which helps us integrate new learning.

We may experience many kinds of shimmering moments. Significant life events such as birth and death are deeply spiritual experiences. Such milestones may lead to a moment of spiritual awakening or insight because they compel us to pause and reflect on life's greater meaning and potentially arrive at insights that help us live more fully and with a greater sense of purpose. Though we often can get caught up in our emotions when these shimmering moments occur—the joy of welcoming a new pet into our home or the sorrow we feel when we lose a pet—subsequent self-reflection on these milestones can lead to life-changing insights.

In addition to insights gained through self-reflection, our dreams may also be an important source of spiritual learning and growth. Sometimes our dreams are prescient and help us make important decisions during times of transition, especially when a solution to a problem has eluded our waking minds. Personally, I've had many dreams that seemed like premonitions, and these dreams are central to my spiritual journey.

Our dreams are also often filled with images and symbols that, at first glance, may be difficult to understand. Yet when we reflect on them, we might begin to appreciate their connection to the events in our lives and gain insight into their significance. Dreams may also be intensely emotional. We may be filled with joy and love, though we may also experience fear, foreboding, and anger—painful emotions that we struggle to fully engage with when we're awake. Not all dreams are spiritual in nature, but over the years, I've learned to pay attention to my dreams, particularly those that have stuck with me over time and evoke a particularly strong emotion.

Our spiritual experiences may also emerge through mysterious, uncanny coincidences that seem to defy a logical explanation. Imagine you receive an unexpected phone call from an old friend at the precise moment you're thinking of them, even though you haven't thought about that friend in years. Or maybe a stray cat shows up on your doorstep just as you're looking through online listings for cat adoption. I refer to such events as moments of synchronicity, and they raise the tantalizing question of whether unknown forces are at work in our lives.

Finally, our spiritual experiences often occur when we're immersed in nature. Such experiences appear to be universal to all people, although they can be difficult to capture with words. For example, we might feel awe and wonder when we witness a glorious sunset, but no matter how hard we try to describe what we felt in that moment, words don't seem to do it justice. Eco-theologian Thomas Berry reminds us that rich spiritual experiences in the natural world put us in touch with the great connection between "the wild and the sacred."[7] He also calls on us to recognize that if we disrespect this connection, we become spiritually impoverished. As Berry writes, "Without the soaring birds, the great forests, the sounds and coloration of the insects, the free-flowing streams, the flowering fields, the sight of the clouds by day and the stars by night, we become impoverished in all that makes us human."[8]

In our complex, increasingly urban world, many of us have discovered that our strongest connection to the magnificence of the greater-than-human world lies in the company of our animal companions. And just as we might struggle to capture the quality of our spiritual experiences in nature with words, many of us also struggle to find words that capture the quality of the relationships we enjoy with our heart animals. Remember Lillian's reflections on the inexplicable yet powerful sense of connection she felt when she first met her cat Freddie? "I was not expecting to get a cat that day," she said. "In fact, it was the last thing on my mind. I was just dropping off my recycling, and something told me to go into the shelter. And that's when I saw Freddie. Our eyes met, and it was like he called to me. I can't explain it.

He was the only cat I looked at that day. . . . He was my cat right from the start. I think we were meant to be together. It was an immediate bond." On that memorable day, Lillian met her animal soulmate, and her life would never be the same.

My hope is that by examining your experiences with animals through the lens of your personal spirituality, you'll gain a greater appreciation for all that is sacred to you. The spiritual journey offered by the learning series provides a rare opportunity to explore your bonds with your animal companions by considering diverse aspects of your spiritual life, including your beliefs in a higher power or universal life force, the way you find meaning, and the continual creation of your authentic personal identity. You'll be asked to call forth all the "shimmering moments" that have defined your love for animals. In doing so, you may discover new things about yourself and envision new directions for your life.

CHAPTER 14

A Roadmap for
Your Spiritual Journey

In my work as a veterinary chaplain, I developed an approach to spiritual caregiving that I call the 3 Chaplain Cs Method of Storytelling™, or the 3 Chaplain Cs, for short. This method includes three primary domains: connecting with your loved one, coping creatively with the loss of that loved one, and communicating with others about the loss. In *Veterinary Chaplaincy,* the final book in the learning series, I'll describe how this method is used in pastoral care conversations with grieving pet keepers. At this point in our journey, however, we'll use the 3 Chaplain Cs as a tool for self-discovery.

In the introduction, I noted that as the first book in the series, this volume sets the stage for a spiritual journey through pet keeping and loss. The three domains of the 3 Chaplain Cs represent the major touchpoints of this journey, and the series is organized according to these three domains, providing a simple roadmap for your spiritual journey. As you make your way through the next two books in the learning series, you'll delve deeply into each of these domains. For example, the second book in the series, *Always in My Heart,* explores the powerful connections we enjoy with our animals (the first domain) and also describes the grief journey we undertake as we struggle to cope with the loss of a pet (the second domain). The third book, *Just an Animal*, explores the social and cultural context of pet keeping and loss in contemporary Western society (the third domain). In this chapter, I'll briefly describe the method's three domains to give you some insight into the journey ahead.

Before we begin, I'd like to note that spirituality is not included as a separate domain in the 3 Chaplain Cs framework, primarily because it's present in all three domains. As we saw in the previous chapter, our spiritual beliefs are central to our sense of intimate connection with other living things, whether human or animal. Many people describe their pets as their "soulmates" or "spirit friends," and some consider them spirit guides who offer important lessons about love, tolerance, and forgiveness. Our spirituality also plays a critical role in our ability to cope with losing a loved one as we struggle to make sense of our loss. Coping with loss is an emotional challenge, but it is also a spiritual challenge, and many people turn to their spiritual or religious beliefs for comfort and guidance. Finally, our families' and communities' collective spiritual beliefs inevitably shape our own beliefs. When others love what we love, we may feel spiritually uplifted. When others fail to understand or appreciate what we care about, we may question our spiritual beliefs and the validity of our sense of spiritual connection with a lost pet.

With only three areas of concern, the 3 Chaplain Cs may seem to be an overly simplistic way of framing a complex experience. But I have found it to be a powerful tool for helping us make meaning of our relationships with our animal friends. I've been using this method for years with great success, and I have yet to find any aspect of the pet loss experience that doesn't fit within this framework.

I also used the 3 Chaplain Cs in my interviews with the vet tech students, and the rich meanings these students made of their interactions with their heart animals are a testament to the efficacy of this interview framework. All the students were able to articulate the profound ways their animals shaped their lives and the lessons they learned from them. For example, John learned that the nonjudgmental love he received from his childhood dog Dare was essential to surviving his troubled childhood and youth. Kelly learned a similar lesson and also believed that animals are our guardians and spiritual guides. Frank's relationship with his cat Muppet transformed his perspective about all animals and helped him understand that they teach us many life lessons and deserve a high quality of life. Every pet story in this book offers similar insights, and I've learned that the 3 Chaplain Cs method encourages people to consider every aspect of their experiences with their animals, including the quality of their connection with a pet, what helped and hindered their coping, and their social experiences.

I believe this method will help make your experience of pet keeping and loss more understandable. As you go through the series, the learning resources in each book will encourage you to reflect carefully on the method's three domains. When you complete the first three books in the series, you'll have a deeper understanding of the powerful ways your heart animal (or animals) has shaped your life, your values, and your spiritual identity.

The First Domain:
Connecting with Your Loved One

The first domain of the 3 Chaplain Cs concerns the quality of the relationships we enjoy with our animal friends. Almost every pet keeper I've ever met has commented on how their animal loved them unconditionally and offered companionship and support during difficult times in their lives. In the company of our pets, we can set aside our social personas and simply be ourselves, without the pressure to perform or please others. The physical closeness we enjoy with our animals is also an important part of the bond, and their amusing, adorable antics can make our days lighter and more enjoyable. Our animals also teach us how to embrace each moment with joy and see the world through a child's eyes. Many pet keepers simply enjoy having an animal to nurture and care for, fulfilling their need to be needed. We enjoy all these remarkable benefits as well as many other gifts in the company of our animal companions.

The vet tech students mentioned many of these qualities when they talked about their heart animals. Most discussed pets they'd kept in childhood and described their animals as their best friends or siblings. For example, Rachel fondly recalled the games she and her sister played with her dog Raffi, and she credits that affable yellow lab with "teaching her a sense of friendship." Colleen also enjoyed a wonderful friendship with her childhood dog Pretzel, who used to perch on the handlebars of her bicycle as she rode around her neighborhood. "Everyone would laugh because he was so cute," Colleen recalled. "He loved it. He didn't want to get down." And Mollie described her horse Honey as her best friend. "To me, animals aren't just animals," she said. "They're your friend. They're your better half sometimes. That's what Honey was for me. That horse loved me to death, and I loved her."

Other students regarded their pets as babies or children and greatly enjoyed caring for them. Frank was one of these doting pet parents. "I took care of Muppet, from feeding her with an eyedropper when she was a tiny kitten to the time she passed away," Frank said. "It was an entire life of learning and watching. . . . I made an effort to make sure she had a good life with the best foods, appropriate exercise, regular vaccinations, and limiting her exposure to illness."

As previously noted, the first domain of the 3 Chaplain Cs is explored in greater depth in *Always in My Heart*. Of all the books in the series, *Always in My Heart* deals most directly with the unique quality of person-pet relationships, giving you the opportunity to reflect on all the gifts you've received from your animal friends and the lessons you've learned.

The Second Domain:
Coping Creatively with the Loss of Your Loved One

The love we feel for our pets remains when we lose them. We continue to love them long after they're gone, and these connections are more than mere memories. They are cognitive, affective, physical, and spiritual connections—bonds of the mind, heart, body, and soul. You may feel sorrow when you think of your pet's death or loss, but in time the happiness and joy you felt in their company will once again fill your heart. Physically, you might experience a feeling of warmth in your chest or the soft whisper of your pet's fur against your skin. As Frank observed, "I can still feel Muppet rub up against my leg. I can actually *feel* her. . . . I constantly see her. I don't even have to close my eyes, and I can see her. Even though Muppet is gone, she's still with me all the time in heart and spirit."

You might also experience a continuing spiritual connection with your pet and hold fast to the hope that you will one day see your animal friends again in the afterlife. For Celeste, her belief that all her lost animals were waiting for her in heaven was very comforting. "Someday, I'll see all my animals that have passed," she said. "I'll have my dachshund, my guinea hens, my rabbits, cats, dogs, ferrets, fish, and any other animals I've had. . . . To hear Rambo say, 'I understand, and I love you' would be the best thing that could ever happen."

Like Celeste, many people turn to their spiritual or religious beliefs when a loved one is lost. Our spiritual stories—or the way we conceive of the cosmos, our place in it, and our relationship with other living beings—play a critical role in our ability to cope with the loss of a loved one. The narratives offered by the world's major faith traditions provide a comforting vision for what happens to us after death, promising that death is not the final act. Some traditions assure us that we will be reunited with our deceased loved ones in a spiritual realm free of pain and suffering.

As discussed earlier, however, you don't have to participate in organized religion to lead a rich spiritual life and draw comfort from your belief in a spiritual realm. Kelly said she wasn't "super religious," but she still thought of her dog Zuzu as her "guardian angel." "I think that animals were placed here by a bigger force, whether it be God or whatever else, to comfort humans," Kelly said. "If you take the time and energy to care and make a connection with an animal, they really are your heart and soul, and I think they really do guide us."

People nurture a continuing connection with their lost pets in a variety of ways. Saving keepsakes is especially common, like the old set of horseshoes that Mollie planned to hang on her wall or the chewed-up soccer ball that Caroline wanted to hold on to because it reminded her of her dog Jamie. Lillian said that Freddie's picture is one of her most cherished possessions. "I still have his pictures up," she said. "I just moved, and I was unpacking things this weekend, and that was one of the first things that went up on the bookshelf—Freddie's picture. I still love Freddie, and I always will."

For many of us, the loss of a pet is one of the most painful events of our lives. Yet I'm continually amazed by the imaginative ways people find to memorialize their pets and, in doing so, maintain a healing connection with their animal. I'm also impressed by the resilience of the human heart. Even after the most tragic losses, I've witnessed people bounce back with a renewed sense of purpose in life and a deep desire to honor their pet's legacy. This transformation takes time—sometimes a lot of time. But in the long run, the loss of a pet can emerge as a "shimmering moment" that marks a positive turning point in our lives.

Always in My Heart explores these ideas and more. By framing the loss of a beloved animal as part of our spiritual journey, we can view it as an opportunity for new learning and personal growth. Some of our most difficult experiences may also be the most instructive. With time and effort, great sadness can be transformed into great joy and true wisdom. As the Sufi poet Rumi said, "The wound is where the light enters you. Any pain you may feel is a messenger; listen to it."[1]

The Third Domain:
Communicating with Others About Your Loved One

In Western society, many of us are accustomed to thinking of grief as an internal psychological experience or something that occurs only in the mind and heart of a single individual. However, we're highly social creatures, so our view of the world and how we process our experiences and find meaning is inevitably shaped by our social interactions. Our social lives are central to our well-being. When we enjoy meaningful social connections, we experience high self-esteem. But when we lack them, we may feel isolated and alienated, and our self-esteem may suffer.

Pet loss is widely minimized in Western society, and the unspoken expectation is that we should return to normal quickly and quietly after losing a pet. Some people may suggest, for example, that you'll feel better if you get another pet, as if one animal can easily replace another. They may also question why you might grieve for a pet for more than a few weeks. These social signals can be so pervasive that you might be inclined to hide your feelings. You might even come to believe that you shouldn't grieve at all for your pets, even when your heart is broken.

When we lose a loved one, the sympathetic support we receive from others—or the lack of support—impacts our capacity to cope. The stories in this book demonstrate the truth of this observation. Some students were surrounded by supportive friends and family, including John, Kelly, Frank, Jane, Caroline, and Colleen, and all said that the sympathetic support of their family and friends was comforting and helpful. When her childhood dog Zuzu died, for example, Kelly said she took it hard, but that her mom "picked me up and took me to the rocking chair, where I curled up in a little ball again and cried some more. My sister and brother were really supportive because they could see how upset I was, and they were upset too." Frank also commented on the support of his family and friends when his cat Muppet died. "She's buried out in the forest with several other animals," Frank said. "A gentleman I used to work for owns fifteen acres out in the forest, and that's where some of our animals are buried together. . . . I felt like I had good support when she died—primarily from my mom and also the people I worked with. I'm thankful for that."

The experiences of Mollie, Rachel, and Celeste paint a starkly different picture. All struggled to find support among their family and friends when they lost their heart animals. Mollie's parents buried Honey without giving her the opportunity to say goodbye, and she said that her family and friends "couldn't really understand why I was so upset." Rachel said that her parents were never really "pet people" and that "it was hurtful because I thought about animals differently than they did." Celeste also commented on the lack of support when Rambo died because he was neglected by her ex-husband. "Nobody really understood how I felt after Rambo died," she said. "There was nobody who would talk to me. I wasn't close to my mother, and she wasn't an animal person. My sisters would just say, 'Well, you'll get over it. Get another pet.' Or friends would say, 'Yeah, I'm sorry you're going through this, but you'll get over it.' And that's about all I heard. There was no consolation."

Overall, our society seems to be moving in a direction of recognizing pet loss as a serious concern. I've met many people whose family, friends, and coworkers made a point of reaching out, sending cards or flowers, listening to their stories, and helping them plan a memorial for their pet. Sadly, however, I continue to encounter people who lack social support when they lose a pet. Most pet keepers appear to have mixed social interactions when they lose a pet. This is one of the primary reasons I created the Pet Chaplain Learning Series. As a veterinary chaplaincy educator, I'm striving to teach as many people as possible about the power of the human-animal bond, the intense grief many of us experience when we lose a pet, and best practices for helping each other feel heard and understood.

The third domain of the 3 Chaplain Cs reminds us to think about our pets as a part of our social world rather than separate from it. Even when your relationship with your pet is highly personal, experienced only by you, your feelings about that relationship may be influenced by the perspectives of the people in your life and the messages you receive about animals in society. We'll explore these topics in greater detail in *Just an Animal*, which offers a deep historical perspective on the evolving human-animal bond.

Discussion Questions

1. Describe an occasion when a story that's sacred to you felt "stuck in your throat." Who were you with, what were the circumstances of the occasion, and what made you feel that you couldn't share your story?

2. Now describe a time when you felt comfortable sharing a story with someone. Who were you with, what were the circumstances of your conversation, and how did that conversation make you feel?

3. In chapter 13, we explored various ways that we express our spirituality. Describe at least one important spiritual experience in your life. This might be a major life event, a powerful dream, a moment of synchronicity, or an experience of awe and wonder. What meanings do you make of this experience?

4. Answer the following questions about Mollie's story in chapter 5. Cite examples from the story to support your answers. You can also include your overall impression of Mollie, how her story made you feel, and any other observations you'd like to share.

   a. *Connecting with a loved one (domain one):* What words did Mollie use to describe Honey? What role did Honey play in Mollie's life?

   b. *Coping creatively with the loss of a loved one (domain two):* What coping strategies did Mollie use to manage her grief? For example, what activities did she engage in to memorialize Honey? What lessons did Mollie learn from Honey and her other animals? How did Mollie's interactions with animals influence her sense of personal identity and life goals?

c. *Communicating with others about a loved one (domain three):* Characterize and describe how Mollie's family and friends responded to her when Honey died. Did their responses help or hinder Mollie's ability to cope with Honey's death? How do you think the social interactions with her family influenced Mollie's grief journey?

The Sacred Story Project

CHAPTER 15

Crafting Your Sacred Story: An Introduction

A sacred story is a personal narrative that speaks to your deeply held values and beliefs and your sense of meaning and purpose in life. Its purpose is to honor your life experiences and explore some simple yet challenging questions: What are your core values and beliefs about animals and the natural world? How have these values and beliefs been shaped by your experiences with animals and the important people in your life, and, conversely, how have they continued to shape your interactions with animals and other people? More broadly, why are you here on Earth and in the cosmos? In other words, why do you do what you do?

Responding to these queries will require you to reflect on your journey thus far and attempt to tease out the meanings hidden in your life experiences. This spiraling process can be difficult or even painful. Yet the benefits of this undertaking make it well worth the effort. For example, reflecting on your relationship with a pet you've lost and crafting your sacred story can support the expression of your grief. It can help you make sense of what may seem like a senseless loss, articulate the life lessons you gained from your animal, and inspire you to incorporate those lessons into your daily life. A sacred story is also a wonderful way to honor a pet's memory and celebrate their life. By articulating the enduring impact your animal has had on your life, you'll be better able to draw comfort and inspiration from your memories. Ultimately, your sacred story can help you identify the activities that speak most strongly to you and inspire you to devote more time and attention to the things that fill you with energy and purpose, rather than those that tend to sap your spirit.

The sacred story project is a progressive exercise, meaning that you'll have the opportunity to craft a story—or a series of stories, if you wish—that you work on incrementally as you journey through the series. As noted in the previous chapter, the second and third books in the series—*Always in My Heart* and *Just an Animal*, respectively—address the three domains of the 3 Chaplain Cs Method of Storytelling: connecting with a loved one, coping creatively with the loss of that loved one, and communicating with others about your loved one. Together, these domains offer a helpful structure for reflecting holistically on your experiences with your animal companions. Writing prompts for each domain are included in those books.

Each pet story in this book is sacred, and my hope is that these narratives will inspire you in crafting your own story or series of stories as part of the sacred story project. In the next chapter, I've also included my sacred story that speaks to my interest in veterinary chaplaincy. It concerns my first dog, a beagle mix named Queenie, and her tragic death. Queenie's story was painful to write, and it also may be painful to read. On the face of it, Queenie's story is a tragic tale of a dog's violent death and a young boy's heartbreak. In the context of my life's journey, however, it's a story of love and redemption. I was never given the opportunity to share my feelings about Queenie and her death in my family of origin, so my life's work has been focused on helping other people share their stories about pets they've loved and lost. The sacred story project will help you examine and reframe your own life experiences—including those that are joyful and painful—into a narrative of enfranchisement, self-discovery, resilience, and personal growth.

I encourage you to take your time with the sacred story project. In the modern world, we're accustomed to moving quickly. Yet contemplating how an important relationship or event has impacted your life requires slowing down and dedicating time and effort to self-reflection. Think about your own story deeply enough, and you'll discover a web of crisscrossing strands of people and animals, joys and sorrows, insights and revelations that lie beneath the surface of your life like the complex root system of a forest. Indeed, it can be difficult to clearly understand the connections between the events that happen in your life; the people, animals, and places you've known and loved; the powerful spiritual phenomena that have awakened your sense of the sacred; and the motives that lie beneath your life's calling. With time, attention, and patience, however, I believe it's possible—and necessary—to make these connections so that you'll better understand your spiritual identity.

Most of us are unaware of the slow flowering of our personal identities and values amid the frenetic activity of the modern world. But then something momentous happens that radically shifts our view of the world and reshapes us to our very core. Sometimes these events are easy to recognize—the birth of a child, welcoming a new animal into our family, graduations, marriage, divorce, career changes, a serious illness, and, of course, the death of a loved one. Often, however, we're not aware of the significance of our experiences as they're unfolding, and it's only in hindsight that we can truly appreciate their importance. As noted in chapter 13, these are the "shimmering moments" of our lives, and I encourage you to focus on your own shimmering moments as you engage with the sacred story project. The story or stories you compose might include dreams that were particularly memorable or prescient; moments of inexplicable synchronicity; or times when you felt a particularly strong sense of awe through a sacred connection with your pet.

I also encourage you to explore *any* relationships or experiences you feel are relevant to your spiritual identity. As noted above, we can't completely separate our experiences with our pets from other aspects of our lives—nor should we attempt to do so. The goal of the learning series is, in part, to help you appreciate your connection with the greater-than-human world. Indeed, many people who love animals and grieve their loss also grieve the rapid loss of flora and fauna in the modern age. If you feel moved to write about your sense of connection with a champion tree and the grief you felt when it was cut down, then please feel free to do so.

Your relationship with family members who were especially influential on your life's journey and your beliefs about animals may also be important to consider. Many of the vet tech students I interviewed—such as John, Kelly, and Jane—had family members who shared their love for animals, and these relationships had a profound impact on their identities as animal lovers and healers. Others—such as Rachel, Celeste, and Mollie—struggled to find support in their families of origin, and those challenges profoundly shaped the choices they made in life. Similarly, as you'll see in the next chapter, my interest in veterinary chaplaincy was strongly influenced by my mom, Helen Gierka, and my younger brother, John, who were both big animal lovers.

Finally, I want to emphasize that the sacred story project is a creative endeavor that you should strive to make your own. Although this exercise is grounded in writing practice, feel free to explore and share your sacred story in other creative ways that complement your written work. If you're crafty, for example, you might wish to create a scrapbook of photos and other memorabilia related to your pet or whatever it is you've chosen to write about. Videos, slide shows, and music are also great mediums for capturing our experiences. You might also select or compose poems and prayers or create a ritual that honors your lost loved one. Do what feels right for you.

Suggestions for Composing Your Story

You might be ready to write your sacred story now. Remember, you can always edit whatever you write now after completing subsequent rounds of the sacred story project. If you choose this approach, I recommend focusing on the first domain, or your sense of connection with your loved one. This is a comfortable place to start for most people as they begin to think about a pet or another loved one they've loved and lost. Recalling your happiest memories can help sustain your energy as you begin to explore the loss of that relationship.

Alternatively, you might wish to write a story that's broader in scope and includes aspects of all three domains. Like the pet stories presented earlier in this book and my story about my dog Queenie in the next chapter, you might describe your sense of connection with your loved one, the occasion of your loss, how you coped with that loss, and the social experiences that were particularly influential on your grief journey.

If at any point in this creative process you feel stuck or need some inspiration, the following guidelines, tips, and exercises might be helpful.

Define your guiding purpose

Establishing an overall goal for your narrative may give you some direction. For example, if you'd like to explore your experiences as a pet keeper and animal lover, you might write about one or two special pets. If you're an animal caregiver who works in the veterinary field or animal rescue, you might focus on the relationships and experiences that compelled you to enter your field. If you're interested in the practice of veterinary chaplaincy, you might consider all the relationships and experiences that have brought you here; eventually, you can pull all this work together to create a clear, focused statement about your interest in interfaith spiritual care for pet loss.

Do some brainstorming

If you have trouble deciding what to write about, I suggest making a list of all the relationships and events that you believe have shaped your love of animals and, if you'd like, your interest in the practice of veterinary chaplaincy. Your list might include interactions with special pets, the important people in your life, memorable experiences in nature, significant milestones in your spiritual life, and so on. The entries on your list do not need to be lengthy descriptions but should include as much detail as you need to make sense of them later. This list will provide an at-a-glance summary of the significant relationships and events you may wish to write about.

Next, select a single entry from this list that seems to rise above all the others in significance and make three additional lists about that particular relationship or event that correspond to the domains of the 3 Chaplain Cs. The goal is to jot down every shimmering moment you can recall about your chosen topic and the thoughts and feelings associated with those memories. You can then add to these lists as you make your way through the series and use them as a reference when you begin composing your story or stories now or in subsequent rounds of the sacred story project.

Alternatively, you could create a chronological timeline that includes the same information described here. A timeline can help you reconstruct your memory of key events in your life and see them in relation to one another. It's a great way to get a snapshot of the significant milestones of your spiritual journey thus far.

Some thoughts on revisiting your past

A common bit of wisdom shared by people working on their memoirs is to write from the scar, not the open wound. Time tends to buffer our strong emotions, and we can generally gain a fresh perspective on our losses when our most intense grief has eased. By examining your most difficult losses and other life-changing events after some time has passed, you'll be better able to articulate the lessons they hold for you.

You'll also be better able to attend to others with the knowledge you've gained from self-reflection, which is particularly important if you're interested in learning more about veterinary chaplaincy. In the words of Buddhist author Lodro Rinzler, "Once [our] wound has scarred over, we are in fact the best people to talk to others about how to heal from similar situations, because we have been there and learned from it. We know the pain of that wound well and can hold space for other people to be present to it, without judgment."[1]

If you decide to write about a pet, your instinct might be to choose one you've recently lost, especially if that pet was very important to you. However, it may be best to select a pet who was lost at least three months ago. When I interviewed the vet tech students, they were required to discuss pets they'd lost a minimum of one year before their interview, and it's likely that the powerful meanings they shared with me took many years to emerge. Many people who lost pets in childhood or young adulthood were never given the opportunity to grieve those loss experiences, and a great deal of personal insight and growth can be gained by revisiting them.

Get visual

Visual aids may be helpful throughout the writing process. If you've chosen to write about a pet, looking at pictures or videos of your animal may help jog your memory, especially if that pet was lost years ago. Conversely, if your pet was recently lost, you may find that you're overwhelmed with grief when you look at pictures of them or revisit your memories of your life together. This is natural and normal. Even joyful moments can be difficult to revisit when your loss is fresh and your grief intense. As noted earlier, practice good self-care during this process. Recognize and honor your painful feelings while simultaneously trying to get in touch with the love and joy you have for your lost loved one.

Write from your heart

In the book *Writing Down Your Soul*, author Janet Conner asserts that writing is one of the best ways to make meaning of our experiences and connect ourselves with what she calls the "Divine Voice" of wisdom and understanding that resides in all of us.[2] "There is a Voice inside you," Connor writes. "There is a Voice inside everyone. Whether you hear it or not, the Voice is there. Whether you ask for help or ignore its guidance, the Voice is still there. Waiting. It is waiting for you to stop, if just for a moment, and listen. The Voice is always there, guiding you, encouraging you, loving you."[3]

The sacred story project is designed to help you connect with this voice or, as Conner phrases it, "penetrate the thin wall of consciousness that keeps you apart" from your inner voice.[4] Other activities can help you connect with this voice, including prayer, meditation, time spent in nature, and creative work such as the visual arts, music, and dance. But research has shown that there's something unique about the way our brains are wired that makes the use of language—especially written language—especially effective for discovering new understandings and meaning in our lives.[5]

If writing is difficult for you or you worry that you're not a good writer, you may find that your story flows better when you describe your experiences out loud. Many recording and transcription tools are available to help you quickly convert your spoken story into written form. It may also help to remember that your sacred story doesn't have to be perfect. Relax, let your words flow, avoid editing your story as you go, and see what arises. You might be surprised at what emerges if you release the "Divine Voice" within.

Immerse yourself in a single moment in time

A good way to jump-start your writing process is to focus on a memory about your chosen relationship or experience that feels particularly meaningful to you. You can then expand your story from there. If you decide to write about a pet, this might be the occasion when your pet came into your life or when you shared a special moment or favorite activity with your pet.

You might also wish to engage in the following writing exercise, which is designed to focus your attention on a specific time and place and to put you in a particular scene. It may also help you tap into your divine inner voice. I used this method when composing my sacred story about my dog Queenie, and it proved to be a powerful way to engage with my past, especially because Queenie died when I was a very young child.

In brief, you'll write continuously for a set length of time without stopping. I suggest starting with a full half hour to see how it feels, but you can shorten this time to fifteen or twenty minutes if you wish. As you write, it's essential to turn off your inner critic. Don't worry about grammar, punctuation, or the organization of your story. If writing by hand, don't lift your pen or pencil from the page. Let your mind relax and your thoughts and feelings flow. Write down whatever comes into your mind, even if it seems repetitive or off topic. Include anything that occurs to you, even if it seems unrelated to your story.

To begin the exercise, find a comfortable place to work for thirty minutes without distractions or interruptions. I suggest muting your cell phone or leaving it in another room. Set a timer, take some deep breaths, relax your body, close your eyes for a moment, and bring your selected memory to mind. Try to put yourself in the scene. Start writing. Begin with the physical sensations that arose for you in that moment. What do you see, hear, taste, and smell? What do you feel on your skin? Where are you? What things do you see around you? What time of day is it? What season is it? Is it hot, warm, cool, or cold where you are? Is the wind blowing? Are there others there with you? What happened? Next, write down all the emotions you experienced as this scene unfolded. Were you happy, sad, angry, elated, lonely, or some other feeling, or did you experience a mixture of emotions? When the time is up, take a break, then review what you've written and make any edits you feel are necessary for clarity and narrative flow.

Wrapping it up

After completing a draft of your story, you might decide that you're happy with your story and feel no need to change it. I've found, however, that the editing process can be a learning experience in and of itself. As you review what you've written, other memories, thoughts, and feelings may arise, offering new insights into the meaning of your past relationships and experiences. It can even be helpful to set your story aside for a while and return to it later. The stories we tell about our past lives are always evolving as we experience new things and engage in new relationships. Those narratives are always with us, informing us and guiding us in life. They're forever a part of who we are, and I hope this exercise has helped you see your past experiences and yourself in a new way.

CHAPTER 16

My Sacred Story
as a Veterinary Chaplain

The best portion of a good man's life: his little,
nameless unremembered acts of kindness and love.

— William Wordsworth, *The Peddler, Tintern Abbey*

As of this writing, I am sixty-nine years old, and I reflect frequently on the paths I've chosen and all that I've accomplished (and wished I'd accomplished) in my life. Professionally, I've enjoyed an interesting and eclectic career in communications; I've done everything from technical writing to teaching and videography to speech writing for a state governor. Yet I can honestly say that my veterinary chaplaincy work means more to me than anything I've ever done in my professional life. There's nothing as fulfilling to me as showing up and showing I care to people who need someone to bear witness to their story and acknowledge their love for their animal and their despair for that animal's loss. Because my work has proven to be so deeply meaningful to so many pet keepers, I've found the energy to keep this project going for more than twenty years.

Why do I do what I do? This is an important question for all human beings, and answering it requires a commitment to self-discovery and contemplation. I try not to live in the past, but I'm nonetheless the sum of my past experiences. Every wound I've ever experienced is still with me, but so is the love, and it is this love that I strive to connect with when I think about my past. The people, places, and animals I love are in my heart forever. They're a part of me, and through my veterinary chaplaincy work, I'm paying that love forward to others.

My call to service is related in part to the values I learned in my Christian upbringing. I was raised Catholic, which places great value on service to those in need. I'm no longer religious, but my early Christian education has had a huge impact on my passion for spiritual care and my interest in community service.

My mom, Helen Gierka, also had a big impact on my life and values. My mom was an animal lover who left food out on the back stoop of my childhood home for any animal who wandered by, and many of those animals eventually became permanent members of my large family. Because of my mom's passion for animals, our house was a menagerie of cats, dogs, birds, gerbils, and rabbits. It got a little crowded and crazy at times. I'm the middle child of ten, and every single one of us was loud, boisterous, and perpetually hungry. Yet I learned from my mom's example that love is infinite and generosity is a way of life. My mom died suddenly of a stroke in 1997, and she remains one of the most loving, kind, and generous people I've ever known. I love animals, though I don't consider myself an animal lover in the same way as my mom or some of the people I've met in my service as a veterinary chaplain. To be honest, I'd say I'm more of a people lover, and I'm especially drawn to people who love animals.

Another person who influenced my interest in veterinary chaplaincy was my younger brother John, who died from an AIDS-related illness in a hospice facility near my home in 1998. The loss of my mom and my brother in the span of two years prompted my interest in spiritual care because I recognized how important it is to have someone who will listen to your story when you've lost a loved one. About six years after I lost my brother, I founded Pet Chaplain, a community service and educational organization devoted to spiritual care for people who've lost pets. My mom and brother were both animal lovers, and my desire to help pet keepers is, in part, a way to honor their legacies.

The relationships and events I've just described are the basic plot points of my journey as a veterinary chaplain, but there is far more to my sacred story than this brief overview would suggest. Throughout the learning series, I'll share stories about the animals, people, and other relationships and experiences that have shaped my life's journey. My goal is to give you some insight into who I am and what I value. As your guide on your spiritual journey, I hope to earn your trust and confidence, and the best way to do this is to share my own stories.

I'll begin here with a story about what may be the most influential event of my journey as a veterinary chaplain—the loss of Queenie, my first childhood dog. Like the pet stories presented in this book, my story about Queenie encompasses all three domains of the 3 Chaplain Cs, including my sense of connection with her, the activities I engaged in to cope with her loss, and my social experiences at the time of her death. It also includes my reflections on how her death impacted my life's journey and the lessons I learned from that experience.

For nearly sixty years, Queenie's story was "stuck in my throat." Frankly, we both deserved better than that. My story is Queenie's story, and my life's work is her legacy. So, here's to you, Queenie, my beautiful friend! I miss you and love you still.

Queenie

When I close my eyes, I can still see her—a small beagle mix with a white coat with brown patches, soft floppy ears, a constant smile, and eager, dark-brown eyes. I was three years old, and Queenie and I were the same height, so we literally saw eye to eye. We used to play a special game. I would climb on the backyard swing and kick off my shoes. Queenie would stand in front of me and arch her back in pleasure as I rubbed my bare feet along her spine and at the base of her tail. Her body was warm, and her fur was thick and soft and tickled my feet. She was always ready to play, and we had great fun together.

One sunny Saturday afternoon, my older brothers and I and some neighborhood kids were wrestling in our front yard in the small township of Schaghticoke in upstate New York. It was a glorious summer day, the sun warm and the grass thick and soft. Queenie was there with us as she always was, barking and running in circles around the tumbling children. At some point, she must have run off, but I didn't realize she wasn't with us until I heard screeching tires. I turned to the road in front of our house and watched as Queenie's body disappeared under a car and popped out the back, rolling along the pavement.

"Queenie's been hit!" someone shouted.

We ran to the edge of the road and stared at her body. There was no blood, but she lay still, and her eyes were closed as if she were sleeping.

"I'll get Dad!" yelled Ricky, my older brother, and he ran into the house.

My father rushed into the road, picked Queenie up, and laid her in the grass. The kids gathered around in a circle, heads bowed and silent, the day's games forgotten. I held my breath as my dad moved his hands slowly along Queenie's body. He was a longtime member of our small town's volunteer rescue squad, and I'd seen him do these gentle, probing movements on people who'd wrecked their cars just down the road from where Queenie had been hit.

"Her back is broken," Dad said. He cradled Queenie in his arms and carried her to our back porch, and all the kids paraded behind him in a solemn procession. He paused beside the cellar steps and turned to look at us, the edges of his mouth turned down. "She's suffering," he said softly. "The best thing to do is put her down."

I didn't understand the phrase "put her down," but I knew about suffering. I'd seen it in my family when my baby brother Jody died the year before after an operation to correct a minor congenital condition. I didn't want Queenie to suffer. Suffering is bad, so I thought putting her down must be good.

Dad disappeared down the cellar stairs. When he returned, he was carrying a wooden apple crate, the kind with spaces between the slats. He put Queenie in the crate and carried her to the back of our station wagon. I remember thinking it was good that the crate had spaces for her to breathe and see out.

"Can I come?" my brother Ricky said as Dad climbed into the driver's seat.

"I want to come too!" I piped up.

Dad looked at us for a moment, two little kids with grass-stained knees, then nodded. We scrambled into the car, Ricky in shotgun and me in the back seat. We drove up Route 40 to Mr. Vial's, the village barber and local constable. Dad left the motor running as he strode up the long driveway to Mr. Vial's front porch. I stood on the back seat, pressing my forehead against the window as I watched. Mr. Vial answered the door, and my father talked and gestured toward the car as the red-and-white- striped barber pole spun beside them. When Dad returned to the car, he was carrying what looked like a loosely coiled black belt. As he passed the mysterious bundle through the passenger side window and placed it on the seat beside Ricky, I was transfixed by the patterned black grip and shiny silver trigger peeking out of the leather holster.

As we drove away from Mr. Vial's house, I leaned over the back seat to check on Queenie. She lay perfectly still, but her eyes were half open, and through the slats of the apple crate she caught my gaze. I'll never forget the way she looked at me, her brown eyes liquid, full of pain and fear. But she loved me, I was sure of it, just as I loved her.

Before long, we arrived at a familiar destination: the village dump. For my brothers and me, the dump was a fun place where we enjoyed weekend adventures with Dad. He'd load us boys into the station wagon along with a load of smelly black trash bags. We liked to climb the tall mounds of dirt, throw rocks, and explore the dump's fascinating collection of junk while Dad threw the trash bags into the pit, and bulldozers covered everything with dirt and gravel.

My memory of the scene that unfolded next flashes in my mind's eye, a kaleidoscope of fleeting images and sensations. I remember Ricky and me getting out of the car and following Dad as he carried Queenie in the crate to a small rise on the edge of a steep embankment. I remember looking down into the pit. Its edges were strewn with flowers, plastic wreaths, and faded American flags. There were no bulldozers or people dropping off trash. There were no sounds either—not even a whimper from Queenie. Dad set the crate down on the edge of the pit. He pulled the pistol from its holster, took a few steps forward, and pointed the gun into the crate. I heard a loud bang that made my body jump, and red blood streamed out of the crate. Dad seemed startled too—he'd flinched when the gun went off—but he quickly stepped forward, slipped his toe under the edge of the crate, and flipped it over the bank.

No one spoke on the ride home. We stopped at Mr. Vial's to return the pistol. Mr. Vial was waiting for us at the end of the driveway. He looked into the car, his gaze passing first to Ricky, then to me. His eyes held mine for a moment. Still, no words were spoken.

To my recollection, we never discussed Queenie's death. But I had questions. Where was Queenie? Was she in heaven with my baby brother Jody, who had died just a year earlier? Would I see her again? These questions were never asked or answered. We simply went on with our lives, as many people did in those days, never sharing what we witnessed on that summer afternoon, much less unpacking how it felt or what it meant to us.

I had a nightmare after Queenie died. In that terrible dream, I was playing my favorite swing-set game with her, except that the swing was at the bottom of the pit where she'd tumbled after my father shot her, and a man was standing on the edge of the embankment firing a gun at me. He shot me, but the bullets went straight through without hurting me. Today, I realize that I wasn't old enough to draw a line between Queenie and me. To borrow a phrase from psychology, I had not yet "separated and individuated." Very young children don't see themselves as separate beings from those they love. Queenie was my best friend. She was a part of me. Seeing her shot was like being shot myself.

It wasn't until I began to practice veterinary chaplaincy in my fifties that I asked my brother Ricky what he remembered about that day. He was five when Queenie died, two years older than I was. I thought maybe he had more clarity about where we went and what happened. He told me that we hadn't taken Queenie to the dump but to the Catholic cemetery. When I learned this, my memories of that day—the lack of trash and bulldozers and the presence of discarded flags and flowers in the pit—made sense. Even after all those years, I found comfort in knowing that Queenie wasn't left in a dump but in a place beyond the church cemetery where dead flowers go.

I've sometimes wondered why my father decided to allow his two young sons to witness their dog's bloody euthanasia. Perhaps he was trying to teach us something about life and death. My father was the first-generation American son of Polish immigrants, and he grew up in a tough world, tougher than I've known. In his world, a dog was just a dog, not a young boy's best friend. If I had been in his shoes, I wouldn't have allowed my young children to witness Queenie's violent death, and I also would have talked to them about why I made the decision to end her life. Yet I am not my father, and the way we think about animals and the way we deal with death and grief in our society has changed a great deal in my lifetime.

In October 2019, more than sixty years after the summer day when Queenie died, I finally wrote down what I'd witnessed. I finally cried for my lost friend. With those words and tears, a weight was lifted from my heart, and I felt a wonderful sense of lightness and freedom. One of the most painful experiences of my life—unexamined, hidden beneath layers of time and silence—lost its power over me. In fact, recalling

Queenie's story empowered me. By carefully reconstructing her death with words in as much vivid detail as I could recall, I finally understood how that tragic event shaped who I am and the path I've chosen in life. Although dredging up those memories was painful, there was beauty in finding my voice and telling a story that had never been told.

I also shared Queenie's story with others. When I initially wrote my tale, I was attending an event called "The Gathering" at Wildacres Retreat in western North Carolina. A weeklong celebration of creativity, "The Gathering" invited artists of all kinds to paint, write, craft, compose, drum, and share their work with each other. The writers held readings every night, and I was reluctant to reveal one of the most painful events of my life—on a stage with a microphone, in front of a roomful of people. I knew the waterworks would start afresh. No one relishes that type of public display. But I also knew that sharing my story about Queenie's death would be another step in my healing.

I prepared myself for the evening's readings with a relaxing walk, and I listened attentively to the stories other writers shared. I felt remarkably calm, at least until I stepped up to the podium and my hands began to tremble and sweat broke out on my forehead. I gazed out at the people in the auditorium, most of whom I knew, some I'd never met. In a shaky voice and with tears in my eyes, I read the story I'd written that day, and a sad chorus of "Ohs" swept through the audience as my tale unfolded. Somehow, I managed to get through it and stumble back to my seat on rubbery legs. I can't say I felt better, but I felt a little lighter, as if the dark clouds of that long-buried memory had begun to break up.

When the night's readings were finished, a few people thanked me for sharing my story about Queenie, and some also shared their own pet stories. Like me, they'd suffered when their animals died, and, like me, they'd rarely talked about those losses. I realized then that by sharing Queenie's story, I'd given them an opportunity to reflect on the losses they'd long kept hidden in their hearts. They learned they weren't alone.

That day at Wildacres was a turning point in my life. I realized that Queenie's death was the seed that would one day grow into the creative expression of my soul's purpose: to acknowledge the grief people experience when they've lost a pet, offer comfort where I can, and, above all, listen to their stories. At that point, I'd been working on my pet chaplain project for nearly fifteen years, but it had never been entirely clear to me where the impulse originated. Now, I knew. I knew that Queenie, my best friend when I was a young boy, was still with me, and the connection and love we shared was still very much alive through my service as a veterinary chaplain.

Our Journey Continues

I invite you to continue your spiritual journey in the next book in the Pet Chaplain Learning Series, *Always in My Heart: Coping Creatively with Pet Loss*. We'll discuss the human-animal bond, death, grief, and the unique challenges we face when navigating a pet's death or loss. You'll discover that, although losing our cherished animal friends is painful, the love remains, and this love can help us heal our hearts and transform our lives as we find creative ways to honor our pets' legacies.

Acknowledgments

Many acquaintances, friends, and colleagues have contributed to the creation of the Pet Chaplain Learning Series. First, we'd like to recognize the team of advisors who generously dedicated their time and expertise to this project. Your enthusiasm for our work and unfailing encouragement buoyed our spirits when we felt overwhelmed by the vast scope of this project. A big thanks to Rev. Jayne Helgevold, hospice chaplain and pet foster mom; Eileen Medeiros, a college English professor and pug enthusiast; Rev. Linda Moore, Episcopal priest, chaplain, and lifelong animal lover; Nancy Osborne, retired hospital chaplain and Clinical Pastoral Education (CPE) supervisor; Fran Prem, who plans and coordinates CPE programs in Australia; and veterinarian Christine Scott. We're especially grateful to Fran for her detailed edits and astute feedback and the extra time and care she put into this project.

We'd also like to applaud the contributions of Kim McCool, who founded a pet ministry at St. John Vianney Catholic Church in Bettendorf, Iowa, shortly after completing our course. Kim is doing amazing things in her community and is truly an inspiration to us.

The learning series would not be what it is today without the input of all the students who participated in our veterinary chaplaincy course. Thank you to those who agreed to let us include your stories and reflections, and we'd like to give an extra big shout-out to Bob Coulson, Mary DeRosa, and Cindi Rodriguez as well as North Carolina artist Amy Wald for interviewing with us. By graciously allowing us to share your stories with our readers, you've had a positive ripple effect on all the people who will recognize themselves in your tales. And, of course, the learning series might not exist at all without the vet tech students who shared their stories with us. Their moving tales about your heart animals were the spark that compelled us to create the series.

In addition, we'd like to recognize the contributions of two scholars who are experts in the work of cultural anthropologist Ernest Becker, whose ideas about death anxiety are discussed in the third and fourth books in the series: Daniel J. Liechty, emeritus professor of social work at Indiana State University in Terre Haute, Indiana; and Sheldon Solomon, professor of psychology at Skidmore College in Saratoga Springs, New York.

A big thanks to our family and friends who cheered us on over the years; your interest and encouragement mean the world to us. Thanks also to our friend Nancy Rogers for providing a final proofread on the books. We're especially indebted to our friend Larry Robinson. Larry, far too often, we ended up bending your ear as we mulled over the many decisions we needed to make in creating an online course followed by a book series. Your stalwart support and friendship—and the many fine dinners we enjoyed in your company—helped sustain us through this challenging journey.

Finally, and most important of all, we'd like to thank the many animals who've touched our lives and helped us become better people.

About the Authors

Rob Gierka holds a bachelor's degree in rhetoric and communications from Albany State University, a master's degree in technical writing from Rensselaer Polytechnic Institute, and a doctoral degree in professional and continuing adult education from North Carolina State University with a research focus on the human-animal bond and pet loss. Professionally, Rob enjoyed an eclectic career in communications, serving in various positions in private and public institutions before retiring in June 2016. He got his start in chaplaincy in the early 1990s when he took an extended unit of Clinical Pastoral Education at Rex Hospital in Raleigh, North Carolina, where he subsequently served as a volunteer chaplain for two years. While in training, Rob also served for a year as a Stephen Minister and for three years as chair of the congregational care committee at Pullen Baptist Church in Raleigh. In 2004, he launched the Pet Chaplain organization and began providing interfaith spiritual support to pet keepers in his community. Between 2004 and 2006, he served as the on-call chaplain at the Veterinary Teaching Hospital at North Carolina State University, and in 2006 he launched a pet loss support group at the Raleigh location of the Society for the Prevention of Cruelty to Animals.

Rob's life partner and coauthor Karen Duke holds a bachelor's degree in English from the University of Florida. She enjoyed a successful career as a writer and graphic designer before retiring in October 2021 and devoting her talents to the development of the learning series.

Notes

Chapter 2: John and Dare

1. Milan Kundera, *The Unbearable Lightness of Being* (HarperCollins, 2005), 297.

Chapter 3: Kelly, Daisy, and Zuzu

1. Martin Buber, *I and Thou* (Scribner, 1958), 96–97.

Chapter 12: The Healing Power of Storytelling

1. Patrick Rothfuss, *The Name of the Wind* (Astra Publishing House, 2007), 658.

2. Janice W. Nadeau, "Meaning Making in Family Bereavement: A Family Systems Approach," in *Handbook of Bereavement Research: Consequences, Coping, and Care*, eds. Margaret S. Stroebe, Wolfgang Stroebe, and Robert O. Hansson (2001): 329–347, https://psycnet.apa.org/doi/10.1037/10436-014.

3. Rachel Park and Kenneth Royal, "A National Survey of Companion Animal Owners' Self-Reported Methods of Coping Following Euthanasia," *Veterinary Science* 7, no. 3 (2020): 89, https://doi.org/10.3390/vetsci7030089.

4. Mary Rose O'Reilley, *Radical Presence: Teaching as Contemplative Practice* (Boyton/Cook Publishers, Inc., 1998), 25.

Chapter 13: Defining Human Spirituality

1. Elizabeth J. Tisdell, *Exploring Spirituality and Culture in Adult and Higher Education* (Wiley, 2003).

2. Elizabeth J. Tisdell, *Exploring Spirituality and Culture in Adult and Higher Education*, 28.

3. John A. Sanford, *Healing and Wholeness* (Paulist Press, 1977), 6.

4. Elizabeth J. Tisdell, *Exploring Spirituality and Culture in Adult and Higher Education*, 32.

5. Elizabeth J. Tisdell, *Exploring Spirituality and Culture in Adult and Higher Education*, 67.

6. Pamela A. Hays, *Addressing Cultural Complexities in Practice: A Framework for Clinicians and Counselors* (American Psychological Association, 2007).

7. Thomas Berry, *The Great Work: Our Way into the Future* (Bell Tower, 1999), 200.

8. Thomas Berry, *The Great Work*, 48.

Chapter 14: A Roadmap for Your Spiritual Journey

1.   Shahram Shiva, ed., *The Essential Rumi Quotes: Top 300 Most Inspiring* (Rumi Network), 72, Kindle.

Chapter 15: Crafting Your Sacred Story

1.   Lodro Rinzler, as quoted in Liza Kindred, *Eff This! Meditation: 108 Tips, Tricks, and Ideas for When You're Feeling Anxious, Stressed Out, or Overwhelmed* (Rock Point, 2019).

2   Janet Conner, *Writing Down Your Soul: How to Activate and Listen to the Extraordinary Voice Within* (Mango Media, 2021).

3.   Janet Conner, *Writing Down Your Soul*, 7.

4.   Janet Conner, *Writing Down Your Soul*, 7.

5.   Janet Conner explores the science that supports the power of writing to help us gain new insights in a chapter titled "Why Write?" in *Writing Down Your Soul*.

Selected Bibliography

Conner, Janet. *Writing Down Your Soul: How to Activate and Listen to the Extraordinary Voice Within*. Mango Media, 2021.

Nadeau, Janice W. "Meaning Making in Family Bereavement: A Family Systems Approach." In *Handbook of Bereavement Research: Consequences, Coping, and Care*. Edited by Margaret S. Stroebe, Wolfgang Stroebe, and Robert O. Hansson (2001): 329–347. https://doi.org/10.1037/10436-014.

O'Reilley, Mary Rose. *Radical Presence: Teaching as Contemplative Practice*. Boyton/Cook Publishers, 1998.

Park, Rachel, and Kenneth Royal. "A National Survey of Companion Animal Owners' Self-Reported Methods of Coping Following Euthanasia." *Veterinary Science* 7, no. 3 (2020): 89. https://doi.org/10.3390/vetsci7030089.

Tisdell, Elizabeth J. *Exploring Spirituality and Culture in Adult and Higher Education*. Wiley, 2003.

Index